EXPLORING
HEAVEN

EXPLORING
HEAVEN

What Great Christian Thinkers Tell Us
About Our Afterlife with God

ARTHUR O. ROBERTS

HarperSanFrancisco
A Division of HarperCollins*Publishers*

EXPLORING HEAVEN: *What Great Christian Thinkers Tell Us About Our Afterlife with God.* Copyright © 2003 by Arthur O. and Fern L. Roberts Family Trust. All rights reserved. Printed in the United States of America. No part of this book may be used or reproduced in any manner whatsoever without written permission except in the case of brief quotations embodied in critical articles and reviews. For information address HarperCollins Publishers, Inc., 10 East 53rd Street, New York, NY 10022.

HarperCollins books may be purchased for educational, business, or sales promotional use. For information please write: Special Markets Department, HarperCollins Publishers, Inc., 10 East 53rd Street, New York, NY 10022.

HarperCollins Web site: http://www.harpercollins.com

HarperCollins®, ▲ ®, and HarperSanFrancisco™ are trademarks of HarperCollins Publishers, Inc.

FIRST EDITION

Designed by Kris Tobiassen

Library of Congress Cataloging-in-Publication Data is available on request.

ISBN 0-06-053068-5 (hardcover)

03 04 05 06 07 ❖/QUE(M) 10 9 8 7 6 5 4 3 2 1

To my beloved wife, Fern

CONTENTS

ACKNOWLEDGMENTS IX

FOREWORD *by David Brandt* XI

INTRODUCTION *by Richard J. Foster* XIII

ONE   What Is Meant by "Heaven"? 1

TWO   Where Is Heaven Located? 12

THREE   What Does *"Eternal* Life" Mean? 35

FOUR   Evidences for Heaven 62

FIVE   The Inhabitants of Heaven 84

SIX   What Sort of Persons Will We Be? 100

SEVEN   Activity in Heaven 112

EIGHT   Society in Heaven 129

NINE   The Renewed Cosmos 151

CONCLUSION 167

EPILOGUE 171

APPENDIX A   Biblical References to
Resurrection and Eternal Life 173

APPENDIX B   "General William Booth
Enters into Heaven" *by Vachel Lindsay* 183

ANNOTATED BIBLIOGRAPHY 187

NOTES 213

ACKNOWLEDGMENTS

I acknowledge with appreciation the support of George Fox University colleagues. The manuscript circulated among faculty in the religion department, and I am especially grateful to Thomas Johnson, Paul Anderson, Howard Macy, Ron Woodward, Phil Smith, and Denise Waterer for their comments. Smith, the logician, encouraged me to make the text evocative as well as orderly. Anderson helped with biblical interpretation. From the science department, Dwight Kimberly and Robert Harder read the manuscript at various stages and offered constructive criticism. Harder asked probing questions about the relationship between eternity and time. President David Brandt, himself a physicist, clarified scientific issues and agreed to write a Foreword. A missiologist friend and fellow poet, Nancy Thomas, offered helpful editorial suggestions. I am grateful to longtime friends Mary and David Jaquith for a discerning reading of an early draft, and for their encouragement. Yachats friends and neighbors Jim and Jan Burley, Philip and Mary Evelyn King, and Erman Mays read the manuscript and offered helpful input, as did James Howe, pastor of the Waldport, Oregon, Presbyterian Church.

Through their writings, Thomas Oden of Drew University and Carol Zaleski of Smith College reinforced my understanding of historic, centrist, Christian theology. They readily granted permission for several citations from their writings, and offered their encouragement.

A writer on Christian spirituality, Richard Foster, has been a great encourager for his former teacher. For many years he and I have shared thoughts on Christian themes and prospective writing projects. I very much appreciate his friendship and his support for this book.

Steve Hanselman of HarperSanFrancisco, and his assistant editor, Julia Roller; production editor Lisa Zuniga; copyeditor Kathy Reigstad; and designer Kris Tobiassen offered constructive editorial and design assistance in a friendly and supportive spirit. Their assistance is very much appreciated!

My wife of sixty years, Fern, has provided emotional support during arduous writing sessions as well as offering practical suggestions for improving the text.

FOREWORD

As a physicist, I have long been intrigued by the cosmos—its size, its complexity, and its apparent "unknowableness." As a Christian, I have often asked myself the questions Arthur Roberts asks in *Exploring Heaven:* Of what sort of reality does heaven consist, who will be there, and where is heaven located? If the universe is all the space available to anyone for anything, then where in this universe is heaven?

Not so long ago, scientists were convinced that the universe was well understood. Then, in the twentieth century, physicists occasionally had questions for which the answers proved elusive. How many dimensions are there, and why are we limited to experience only three (or four, if one includes time)? The world of Harry Potter, which allows persons to gain access to another world on track nine and a half, is pure fantasy. But might there be dimensions with which we are unable to connect directly while in this life? Roberts suggests that a "new body might well move through space and time differently from before, but somehow similarly." The resurrected body might find track nine and a half, even when it would be entirely impossible during our current lives.

The concept that there is continuity of some sort between this world and the next is rather appealing to this physicist, who is pleased when large-scale phenomena, such as human bodies moving, are continuous in nature.

The basic principle that heaven will be a lot like life as we experience it now, here on earth, is an attractive view of life after death. The concept is supported by comparisons of heaven and earth, as, for example, in the Lord's Prayer. It affirms the goodness of God's creation, especially the high value of humans—so valuable as to warrant God's Son being sent to live as an example for us and then to give his life to allow us to gain eternal life.

To think of life in heaven requires some imagination, because there is much mystery about heaven, much we do not know. Arthur Roberts depends on a strong scriptural base and careful thinking to provide a fresh, wonderful picture of heaven—that great, real place that has provided hope for the saints throughout the ages.

—DAVID BRANDT

INTRODUCTION

I am struggling to find a way of explaining to you how very much I like *Exploring Heaven*. Maybe it would help you to know of my initial reluctance about the subject matter itself. I worried that a topic like heaven is simply too antithetical to the prevailing materialism of our age. I was concerned that such a book might make us, as the saying goes, "so heavenly minded that we are no earthly good." I wondered about how much we can really know about a reality that lies beyond the direct experience of any of us.

Well, my concerns were quickly put to rest. Even more, I became genuinely intrigued, eager to see where each new chapter would take me. For me, Arthur Roberts rescued the subject of heaven from both the radical skepticism and the superstitious fads of modern culture. I believe he can do the same for you.

If you have ever wondered whether the idea of heaven is merely a theoretical human construct, then this book is for you. If you have ever entertained doubts or questions about a future existence after this life, then this book is for you. If you have ever thought of heaven's residents as rather dull, ethereal beings perched on billowing clouds strumming golden harps, then this book is for you. If you have ever imagined heaven to be simply one never-ending worship service, then this book is for you.

Both biblically and historically informed, *Exploring Heaven* discusses intelligently and wisely a huge array of topics that perplex us whenever we think about heaven. The reasons I like it are myriad. I mention four.

First, I am taken by the fairness with which Roberts presents the many competing approaches to this topic. We are never in doubt as to where he stands on the matter at hand, but we always feel that other options receive an honest representation. Whether Freudian, Marxist, social Darwinist, or otherwise, all are given a fair hearing. So are the various perspectives from great Christian thinkers throughout the ages.

Second, I am impressed by how well he roots his discussion of heaven in the realities of human life here and now. Thankfully, it avoids the escapist "pie in the sky in the sweet by and by" that plagues so many writings in the eschatological genre. In speaking of poets and their prophetic role in society he writes, "They spell injustice in stanzas dripping with blood. They nag us out of indifference. Directly or indirectly, they witness that Eternal City whose architect and builder is God, and by their rhetoric they stir us toward its holiness." On another occasion he notes that "persons of faith . . . do God's will on earth; they are energized by hope and filled with joy. Their works of love and truth leaven the earthly city, making it an anteroom to heaven." This then is a socially informed, realistic discussion of a future reality that is firmly rooted in the rough-and-tumble of the present world.

Third, I am impressed by the unique combination of caution and passion with which Roberts approaches the subject of heaven. At one point he writes, "Certainly a veil separates us from the next world. Exploring heaven isn't an exact science! . . . Like a child waiting to open a Christmas package, one inner voice says, 'Wait, don't peek, let it be a surprise!' while another voice says, 'It won't hurt to examine the package in anticipation of its contents.'

Although we can't peek through the wrappings of God's great gift, there are clues in Scripture and human experience . . . to quicken our excitement. . . . God created us with minds to draw analogies and test intuitions, and with spirits to soar upon the Wind."

The reference to "minds" that are able "to draw analogies and test intuitions" brings me to my fourth, and in many ways my most important, point about this book, namely, its compelling logic. It might help you to know that Arthur Roberts was, and is, my teacher. The history of philosophy is his specialty, and during my college years I took more than one course from him in the field. One of those courses was in logic, and I enrolled in the course even though it was not required. (It is hard to imagine anyone today voluntarily enrolling in a course in logic!) Under Dr. Roberts' careful tutelage I learned about *non sequiturs* and *ad hominem* arguments and all manner of *post hoc* fallacies. Even more important, I learned about the proper use of syllogisms and the difference between deductive and inductive reasoning and the importance of logical inference. And it is in these ways that *Exploring Heaven* shines the brightest. One step at a time it walks us through Scripture, through the history of interpretation, through scientific inquiry, and through the differing approaches and theories, and shows us what we can know, what we cannot know, and what we can logically infer from the biblical record and human experience.

Exploring Heaven is a clear, accessible, hopeful book. If you will give it your sincere attention it will surely bring you, as it has me, into a joyous confidence that we are eternal beings with an unceasing future in God's good universe.

—RICHARD J. FOSTER

ONE

What Is Meant by "Heaven"?

PUTTING IT TOGETHER

I've kept my life as a scientist and as a believer
separate for years. But since my wife died last month
I've been trying to put the compartments together.
My head says Martha is just ashes strewn at sea.
But my heart tells me she lives, somewhere.
Help me sort it out, Lord.

—*Prayers at Twilight*[1]

Heaven isn't something we think about regularly, but it does come to mind, doesn't it? Especially when life-destroying disasters occur, like earthquakes or the September 11, 2001, terrorist attacks upon the United States. Whenever death casts its dark shadow over your life, do you wonder whether, in his delightful books, C. S. Lewis glimpsed a Light beyond the tunnel of death or was just whistling in the dark? Or do you wonder about heaven when you're simply in a thoughtful mood, as you may be now? If so, this may be a good time to join me in pondering what most of the world's people have believed in, or hoped for—a life after this life.

The word *heaven* conveys quite a few meanings. As a religious term, it has been used historically to denote where people go after death. But it has carried other, less religious, meanings, too. It's sometimes employed as jargon for top-of-the-line stuff, like "heavenly music" or "heavenly hash." The word may be selected to connote an idyllic vacation spot. It may be used as a merchandising gimmick, hyping the latest "RV heaven" or designating a place that peddles the ultimate in fashionable accessories. You can find hundreds of such "heavenly" spots on the Internet. Obviously, the word (and the notions it conveys) carries power, or it wouldn't be borrowed so much.

As a result of such borrowings, *heaven* has become such a part of everyday speech that its idiomatic use has obscured root meanings. We must clear away the verbiage of the word's cultural derivatives to understand its full significance. Like classic cars, some words need to be restored. *Heaven* is one such word. Machines made of metal embody excellence of form and function; they endure for a time. Words made of truth, as *heaven* is, embody excellence of form and function. They endure forever.

Contemporary use of the term, even in a narrow sense, also depends on whether (and how) one uses the singular or the plural. Is it *heaven* or *heavens*? Exasperated at a minor annoyance, you might blurt out, "Oh, heavens!" Or, drenched in wonder on a star-studded night, you might murmur lines from a remembered psalm: "The heavens declare the glory of God." We tend to use the singular, *heaven,* to refer to the realm of the afterlife, and the plural, *heavens,* to refer to the sky and everything else out there—which covers scads of stuff and lots of territory, given the billions of galaxies, spiral nebulae, black holes, dark as well as ordinary matter and energy, quasars, WIMPS ("weakly interacting massive particles"), and who knows what else.

Bible language isn't that neatly divided, however. In the Old Testament the phrase "under heaven" more often denotes a cosmic totality. Consider this admonition from Deuteronomy (4:19):

> And when you look up to the heavens and see the sun, the moon, and the stars, all the host of heaven, do not be led astray and bow down to them and serve them, things that the LORD your God has allotted to all the peoples everywhere under heaven.

It has been argued that because ancient peoples were unsophisticated, they located God in the panoply of space "above" them, sometimes picturing gradations, such as "third heaven" or "seventh heaven"; whereas we, with our greater knowledge of stars and planets, should use scientific descriptions instead of religious ones. Well, where would that locate God? Is God just a product of human thought? Of course not! However described, the cosmos is still God's creation. Biblical writers may not have been sophisticated, but they were wise, and they felt awe worshiping Almighty God, "maker of heaven and earth."

Fuller Seminary professor Paul K. Jewett interprets that historic creedal phrase to indicate an inclusiveness in the cosmos, a belief that there is "no qualitative difference between heaven and earth as there is between the Creator and creation," and he cites Psalm 113, in which God's glory is said to be "above the heavens."[2] People in biblical times envisioned the heavens as God's throne, and earth as his footstool. The ancients understood that the whole creation is the Lord's, and, with metaphoric discernment, exulted that God had flung the stars into space. As the prophet Jeremiah expressed it (23:24): "'Who can hide in secret places so that I cannot see them?' says the LORD. 'Do I not fill heaven and earth?'

says the LORD." So whether the ancients referred to rain or manna or commandments coming from heaven, they acknowledged a physical-spiritual unity under divine sovereignty that modern culture, to its detriment, has lost.

The New International Version of the Bible lists 422 entries for *heaven* or *heavens,* 737 for *earth.* Does this ratio suggest that we should give more priority to how and where we live now than how and where we will live later? Sure. But heaven is important, too! Among the various biblical terms translating *heaven(s)* into English, two are central. These are, in Hebrew, *samayim,* and in Greek, *ouranos.* The Hebrews, like other people living in the biblical era, used descriptions of the sky above them both to describe what they saw and to refer metaphorically to the divine order of things. A parallel word, *paradise,* is drawn from the ancient Iranian *pairedaeza*—literally, a garden with a wall. In the Old Testament that word describes both Eden's bliss and the messianic future. In the New Testament it depicts the glory of the resurrected life.

The word *heaven* is used in all of the following ways in the Bible:

- The skies above the earth
- The abode of God
- A synonym for God's will
- The total reality
- The locus of revelation
- The capital of God's kingdom
- The ultimate judiciary
- The repository for prayer petitions
- The place where saints go for eternal life
- The energizing center for natural phenomena
- The standard for righteousness and social order
- The purposive context for historical events

- The archives for good deeds
- The container for modes of existence
- The future reality
- The arena for the struggle between good and evil
- The furnace for reshaping the cosmos

In the modern era science and religion have met at the junction of the singular and the plural, sometimes as antagonists tussling over turf, at other times as allies dividing the territory of reality, the more effectively to explore (or manage) it. In recent decades there's been an uneasy truce in what had been labeled the post-Renaissance "warfare of science and religion." Science takes "the heavens"; religion takes "heaven." Facts go this way; values go that way—separate paths toward separate realities.

Such an arrangement seemed neatly to fit a political separation of state and church. At least it kept the institutions of religion and science from becoming too intrusive. But separating objective (scientific) reality from subjective (religious) reality doesn't work very well. Periodic skirmishes over the teaching of evolution (or creation) in public schools and over whether genetic experiments should occur demonstrate how fragile the truce is. Furthermore, the division is artificial, and it isn't biblical. To an ordered mind a certain mutuality of inquiry and effort is required to achieve coherence in the pursuit of truth. Separate "watertight compartments" don't correlate well with rationality, let alone with a universe of matter and energy.

In recent decades many theologians and physicists have reached "across the divide" in their scholarship, accepting each other no longer as adversaries but now as persons jointly, thoughtfully, and often devoutly exploring a shared and mysterious universe. Several are cited in subsequent chapters and/or noted in the Annotated Bibliography, but I'll highlight a few here: Ian Barbour, who recently retired from Carleton College, is one. His *Religion in an Age of Science* was reedited and published in 1997 as *Religion and Science*. In that book he demonstrates scholarship that creatively incorporates religious passion and scientific acumen. John Polkinghorne, a British physicist and theologian from Cambridge University, is another bridge-builder. This scientist, who in middle age became an Anglican clergyman, aligns these intellectual disciplines along the same spectrum of honest inquiry in books such as *Science and Theology,* and he discovers both human ventures to be humbling before the creation and its Creator. In a recent book, *Why Religion Matters: The Fate of the Human Spirit in an Age of Disbelief,* a renowned scholar of world religions, Huston Smith, addresses the centuries-old warfare of science and religion, which secularists thought science had about won. Smith writes: "Scientific triumphalism has peaked, and hope increases for a peaceful coexistence."[3] I would add that religious triumphalism has also peaked, at least among Christians, although "warlords" in each camp keep sniping at each other in an effort to control turf rights of interpretation.

A social infrastructure has sustained these bridge-builders. In the 1970s a group of Christian colleges supported a program for "the integration of faith and learning" across the curriculum of member schools. The Council for Christian Colleges and Universities has had great impact upon undergraduate students, helping them to correlate faith with liberal arts and professional training. Later in the decade, the Society of Christian Philosophers (of which I am a member) was organized. It has had significant influence within academic institutions both private and public and publishes an influential professional journal, *Faith and Philosophy.* Science-religion colloquia now occur at major intellectual centers across the country, from Berkeley to Boston, and among the academic guilds. A new Center of Theological Inquiry at Princeton University envisions publications aimed at interpreting theology for the twenty-first century. The initial volume, edited by John Polkinghorne and Michael Welker (and cited in this book) is titled *The End of the World and the Ends of God*.

Major foundations serve as patrons for these and other scholarly efforts. They include Lilly, Pew, Murdock, and the Templeton Fund. The latter foundation influences the interface of science and values within elementary and secondary schools, as well as within universities.[4] Many other foundations assist educational programs in science that incorporate not only knowledge and insights acquired through data and technique, but also moral values derived from theology.

In practice, of course, ordinary people routinely bridge the chasm between science and religion. Usually they use the word *heaven* to console friends and neighbors when a loved one dies. To express appreciation for the deceased and to offer hope to the bereaved at a memorial, people typically say something like, "Well, he's in heaven now, dear Uncle Albert, released from all that cancer pain." Or they use euphemisms for the afterlife, such as "with God," or "in a better world."

Have you observed a kind of fuzziness, though, when the word *heaven* and its synonyms are used to depict a future life? Even Easter sermons sometimes treat heaven euphemistically—in a cheery but vague manner, equivalent to saying, "Things are tough now, but don't worry, they'll get better; God is with us, and death isn't the last word." Ah! What an evocative final phrase! If death isn't the last word, what is? How sad if words about heaven are restricted to vague homilies aimed at comforting rather than understanding and interpreting heaven's full meanings.

When we're young and healthy, we raise our eyebrows at fuzzy generalities about the afterlife, craving specifics such as, Will our kitty be there? Because during childhood we're busy living in a present that seems to stretch endlessly before us, we shrug off puzzling questions about the afterlife. That is, until the teen years, when wider experience—especially tragedy—flings into our faces queries about mortality. A middle-school girl is raped and murdered by a neighbor, and friends weeping at the crime scene wonder about heaven and hell. A buddy and his girlfriend take an icy curve too fast and wrap dad's pickup and themselves around a tree—arriving at the morgue instead of at the schoolyard. High-school pals at the cemetery stare wide-eyed at the grave and try to fathom the nature of the afterlife as a preacher proclaims the hope of resurrection.

When we're considerably older—pushing the limits of life expectancy—these questions we had as teens pop up again, nagging us for satisfying answers. Questions that we shoved aside during busy career years when we had enough problems to solve and things to plan and manage in *this* life without bothering our heads over the *next* return to plague us.

As we get older, circumstances force us to face our finitude—emotionally, if not intellectually. They compel us to admit that death will come, and that it will come for *us*. Inevitably, in spite of exercise routines, healthy diet, inoculations, routine mammograms or prostate probes, cataract surgery, hip transplants, bypass surgery, gene therapy, and stem-cell treatments. In quiet moments we admit to ourselves that death is scary to contemplate. Yes, it *is* the final enemy. And so the ultimate question haunts us: But is it the last word?

To reiterate: If death isn't the last word, what is? *Heaven* and synonyms such as *eternal life* hint at the last word, but often they're not spelled out to our satisfaction, even though we prop up our hopes with religious platitudes. Vagueness in the face of a momentous issue makes us uneasy. It prompts hard questions at least, if not easy answers. Do sympathetic mourners and pastors really believe that heaven is a place where our loved ones go and spend forever, a place where one day we will chat with them again, or hug them, argue with them, play games with them, go exploring mountains hand in hand? Or are these comforters just offering oblique and flowery tribute to the deceased and verbal consolation to the mourners?

Look at the pictures of your deceased parents on your bedroom wall. Do you ever wonder, especially on their birthdays, where they are and what they're doing? Is heaven-talk just a nice way to jolt lapsed memory and heighten generational appreciation? Does a suspicion occasionally sneak into your head that such talk is just a kind of cultural socializing, a pious spin on wishful thinking? These spiritual advisors—are they or aren't they talking about a reality out there (or somewhere) and in our future? Are there good reasons to hope for heaven, to anticipate eternal life?

Our swirling thoughts center down to questions such as these: Of what sort of reality does heaven consist? Where, or how, is it located? Who will be there? What is eternal life? What will we be like? What will people do all the time? Where is the universe going?

In this book I probe these and related questions. Chapter Two examines and critiques possible "locations" for heaven and offers the one I find most congenial to the logic of human life, scientific knowledge, and religious teaching. Chapter Three looks at what we mean by "eternal life" and at evidences for it. It considers the polarities of heaven and hell and probes who ends up where, and why. Chapter Four examines evidences for heaven, using the "maps" available to us through human cultural experience. Chapter Five checks out heaven's terrain and its inhabitants, the angels and its horde of immigrants from earth (or elsewhere). Chapter Six probes the nature of personal identity in the afterlife, its problems and characteristics, and the logistical difficulties faced and resolved. Chapter Seven deals with activity in heaven, extrapolating from earthly experiences of work, play, worship, family, socializing, technology, creativity, adventure, and so on to suggest analogous heavenly activities, and seeking to understand space/time reconfigurations. Chapter Eight focuses on society in heaven, anticipating social structures and governance under the Lordship of Christ in a world redeemed from sin. Chapter Nine focuses upon the renewed cosmos, anticipating how God correlates creation with redemption, what it means for the cosmos to be freed from the burden of evil, and how through different dimensions of reality humanity will share in God's dreams for the future.

To accomplish this task I draw upon biblical insights and the interpretations of major theologians from the classic period until the present. I have gained and seek to share with you understandings and insights gleaned from physical and social scientists. Numerous writers, representing different philosophical and religious perspectives, have contributed to my understanding of the subject.

When confronted by mystery beyond the horizon of ordinary life—including the mystery of the afterlife—each of us views that mystery through the faith-lens of a worldview that has brought coherence to our cultural and personal experiences. My worldview is that of a Christian. Accordingly, I find special affinity with Christian scholars past and present, and with the covenants of the Christian faith community. But I have found help from other traditions as well, and from secular scholars who find my faith-position difficult to accept. I am increasingly made conscious that human beings are indeed "of one blood," underneath differences of language, culture, and ethnicity. Our knowledge and our faith lodge within finite beings. As Augustine said, "God is greater in our thoughts than in our words, and greater in reality than in our thoughts." So we learn from each other. I owe much to many writers who doggedly have searched out and sketched the mysteries of eternal life, sharing with us what they've seen, or dreamed, or yearned for, or despaired of, or feared, or hoped.

So I commend to you these thoughtful persons across the centuries whose writings have helped me probe the mystery of heaven. In appreciation to them, and as a help to you the reader, I have prepared an extensive Annotated Bibliography, with apt citations—some works cited within the text, others not. Please consider this an integral feature of the book. I would be pleased if my introduction to these authors led you to read and ponder what they've written.

Exploring heaven actually begins on earth. This is where we live, so we start the journey from where we are, in the here and now. Our minds probe the world about and within us: they interrogate the world we sense; they test the world our reason constructs; they meditate upon the world our intuition envisions and the one we hope for. Our spirits haunt us, especially during times of sorrow and joy, with visions of eternity. The software of eternity lodges in our systems. Ultimately, when words fail to encompass heaven's mystery, we find ourselves silent, awestruck, before the Almighty God, maker of heaven and earth . . . listening, listening.

TWO

Where Is Heaven Located?

Where do we go, oh! where do we go?
Are we dead beyond, or do we yet live?[1]
—*from a fifteenth-century Aztec song*

And if I go and prepare a place for you, I will come
again and will take you to myself, so that where I am,
there you may be also.[2]
—*Jesus*

In this chapter we consider possible "locations" for heaven. Here are some gleaned from observation and from reading about and reflecting on the issue for nearly seventy years. (Oh, yes, I thought about heaven even as a child. Didn't you?)

- Heaven is an illusion; it's not located anywhere.
- Heaven is a reality located in the mind.
- Heaven is a reality located in culture.
- Heaven is a spiritual realm, coexistent with natural reality.

- Heaven is a reality located in the mind of God.
- Heaven is a reality congruent with creation.

This last location of heaven is the one I find the most compelling. I will elaborate it more fully in the chapters of this book. But before considering the evidences available that map heaven as a reality basic to and congruent with the created order, let's first evaluate the insights and the limitations of other proposed views about where heaven is.

LOCATION ONE: HEAVEN IS AN ILLUSION

People who hold this view say that heaven isn't anywhere. They consider the idea an illusion carried over from the childhood of the human race—an illusion that ought now to be cast aside, given our advanced knowledge of the universe and of the human psyche. The lure of "pie in the sky by and by," proponents of this view argue, prevents people from handling personal and social problems constructively. The modern world offers scientific rather than fantastic explanations for realities material and immaterial, they assert. Outer space and inner space alike are to be understood scientifically.

Corliss Lamont supports this view in what has become a classic of modern humanism. Accepting death as an integral part of evolution, Lamont believes, offers freedom from "debasing fear and shallow optimism" and gives greater glory to humanity.[3] Modernity has generally asserted, with Carl Sagan, that "the Cosmos is all that is or ever was or ever will be." (Actually, such a claim is itself a leap of faith, as Huston Smith points out, because it assumes that thoughts and feelings are just expressions of matter. Smith criticizes such reductive naturalism: "Neither materialism nor naturalism is required by anything science has discovered in the way of actual facts.")[4]

Some, following Freud's views in *The Future of an Illusion,* offer psychological explanations for the persistence of what they consider a regressive idea. Others, following Karl Marx, believe the illusion of immortality is a ploy by the elite class, contrived to assure their continued economic dominance over miserable peons or gullible soldiers whom they placate with promises of a wonderful life in heaven. Whether Freudian, Marxist, social Darwinian, or otherwise, avowed atheists consider that the idea of heaven, like other religious notions, is an avoidance technique and should be abandoned for the sake of greater social accountability. They believe in being tough-minded. *Make the most of this life. Accept no guilt trip laid upon humanity by some supposed deity. No escapist fantasy, no wishful thinking.* Like the ancient Stoics, they consider it a mark of human nobility to accept what is rather than pine for what cannot be. *When you're dead you won't know you are, so why worry now? Whatever goes around comes around. After this universe burns up, another may emerge—or may not.* In a more Epicurean fashion some unbelievers urge people to live it up: "Eat, drink, and be merry, for tomorrow we die." The hero of William Henley's *Invictus* speaks for some of them: "I am the master of my fate, . . . the captain of my soul."

Certain evolutionary psychologists and sociobiologists assert that genetic survival is all that matters to the universe. *Nature doesn't give a hoot for happiness. Moral and religious notions are embedded in organic evolution. Genes plus environment dictate the future.* Of course, if viewpoints are biologically determined, their own must be too, which pretty much quashes any value judgments, including the "nobility" of Stoic resignation or the positing of evolutionary purpose!

I wouldn't be writing this book if I accepted these secular viewpoints. But I must acknowledge that occasionally, under stressful circumstances, I have wondered whether heaven might, indeed, be an illusion. I have pondered whether to toss aside a bright hope of eternal life in favor of a supposed "realistic" understanding of the temporal character of nature, including my own personal being in history.

Facing a subtle but fierce secular onslaught against religious faith, must I conclude, wistfully, that religious foundations are crumbling? No, my faith in God is too strong. Both my heart and my head resist this temptation. But I can understand how for some persons the violence of the twentieth century accented a dark reality which for them can more honestly be depicted, with all its horror, without putting deity into the equation. I think that they are mistaken, but I honor their grim determination to "go it alone," to construct purpose and value in a universe which for them seems neither to contain nor to promise either purpose or value.

So it wouldn't surprise me if an old refrain about certainties— "It ain't necessarily so"—has bounced about in your mind from time to time, too. Many persons, especially in Europe and North America, mentally acquiesce that heaven may be an illusion; but emotionally they're not as ready as the tough-minded Stoics to abandon it. They're loath to consider hope of heaven harmful to social order. In fact, they acknowledge the social stability such a hope brings. The heart balks at what the head asserts. Some uneasy agnostics may feel more comfortable at the next level of belief about heaven—as a reality in the mind. Their agonizing doubts may be the flip side of a more credible, but equally anguished, faith. Under pressure from the contemporary "culture of despair," many thoughtful persons are ready to consider how values may indeed be sustained by a heavenly reality.

When the apostle Paul preached to educated Roman pagans about the resurrection of Jesus (with its implications for our own) the historian Luke reported, "When they heard of the resurrection of the dead, some scoffed; but others said, 'We will hear you again about this'" (Acts 17:32). Even secular people have questions about the afterlife that don't go away easily. Some of these persons are also saying, to themselves at least, "We would like to hear about this again."

The next viewpoints are more positive. They claim that the word *heaven* depicts a reality. Proponents believe that mystery points to a divine reality beyond sensory experiences. In varying degrees they affirm theistic interpretations of heaven. They refuse to reduce eternal qualities to chemical or electrical properties. They differ, however, over the *form* of heavenly reality. Over the centuries two concepts of immortality have been in tension. One concept, following Plato, holds that the soul is immortal and, at death, is happily rid of the body. The other, following Judeo-Christian teaching, holds that immortality means the resurrection of the body, which is not an encumbrance, but an essential part of personhood. The following "locations" reflect that tension.

LOCATION TWO: A REALITY IN THE MIND

This first theistic view considers the idea of heaven to be a reality located in the human mind. One could liken it to a conceptual chip implanted by the Creator in the software of the brain, or consider the term a synonym for that concept of perfection essential for moral and aesthetic achievements. In this sense heaven is an ultimate standard against which to test values and to measure self-worth and social order. Heaven thus might be construed as a type of reality lodged within the structures of human consciousness, an ultimate bureau of standards located in the spaces of mind rather than in some government laboratory. In philosophical terms, this view of heaven connotes epistemological rather than ontological reality. In ordinary terms, this view means that heaven exists in mental space, not physical. Heaven is a state of mind, in other words—but a *real* state. An old biblical poet declared that God has set eternity in human hearts even if people "cannot find out what God has done from beginning to end" (Eccles. 3:11). To be created in God's image means having access to eternal qualities.

As a linguistic reality lodged in the human psyche (no mere figment of imagination), heaven is thus construed as a basic tool of human understanding, as vital as concepts such as freedom and generosity. It's a part of self-conscious personhood. When worshipers pray for God's will "on earth as in heaven," they affirm a normative and unshakeable guide to value. Such a mind-set makes people human. Without eternity in the heart, life would lose its purpose, just as a game would lose all meaning without goals and defining rules. In this view heaven is the quintessential norm for human character and achievement.

What about death? Well, this viewpoint espouses altruistic nobility—tender-mindedness. If one follows the heavenly vision faithfully, one bequeaths to those who follow eternal ideals that will keep their lives ordered and creative. Immortality belongs to the human race, and death for the individual is but a gracious stepping aside to make room for others. Following Thomas More's *Utopia*, voluntary euthanasia, espoused by some people (a minority, to be sure), is considered socially responsible when outliving one's own time for death is harmful to others and a burden to oneself. But in any case, according to this view, we've had our turn; now it's time for others to whom God also offers enlightenment—knowledge of the good, a gift that's eternal. Serenity, proponents aver, is best found by affirming this life. They could resonate with the ancient poet Horace (Ode I, 31):

Apollo, grant my prayer,
health to enjoy the blessings sent
from heaven; a mind unclouded, strong;
a cheerful heart; a wise content;
an honoured age; and song.[5]

Admittedly, such idealistic contentment and deference to others come fairly easy if you're pushing ninety, have had a successful and socially responsible career, and enjoy many friends, a loving family, and a dozen bright and upright great-grandchildren. It's more difficult to achieve if you're fifty-eight, recently divorced and "downgraded" from the firm, or twenty-five and diagnosed with terminal leukemia, or eleven and scrounging food from a garbage dump, or fifteen and a bartered and battered sex slave, or thirty-something and about to be hacked to death on a tribal battlefield. It's a bit of a stretch to say that we must all labor harder so such inequalities and evils will diminish, that we must support medical science in order to improve the quality and length of life. But some idealists insist that such "eternity in the heart" is the vision that gathers people to God's kingdom and offers hope for a better life to the individuals who follow us.

LOCATION THREE: A REALITY IN CULTURE

This view expands the notion of heaven beyond the limits of the self. It would have us examine the linguistic origin, beyond individual minds. In this view the word *heaven* signifies a form of reality created in the fertile marketplace of ideas and lodged in that incredibly complex repository of human experience called "culture." Culture encompasses the whole range of human creativity—pop and folk art as well as museum masterpieces, Norman Rockwell and Michelangelo, classical and bluegrass music, opera and high school concerts, hobby clubs and fairs, family picnics and destination resorts, kindergartens and universities, cathedrals and sports arenas, parks and pedestals, commerce and governments. The term encompasses that social edifice, civilization, created by shared human knowledge and skill—a complex mixture across time of ideas, material substances, and action. After all, aren't love and trust and beauty lodged within culture, and don't they possess an eternal quality, beyond what's in individual brains? Just as death doesn't destroy these qualities, neither does it destroy the cultural reality of heaven.

However falteringly, in this view culture embodies the kingdom of God, a realm of reality that moves forward through the rise and fall of civilizations. It transcends the wealth or poverty of societies and the fortunes of war and peace. It embodies eternal ideas basic to scientific and technological achievements, to social institutions, to spiritual and moral values, and to governance—to the human community in general. When you get too cranky about in-your-face-and-in-your-ears television ads and dumb shows, reflect upon the good things culture has done, and how much we all stand on the shoulders of creative people who lived before us. Consider how posterity depends on preserving the ideals that infuse culture with meaning.

If it depended upon me, I couldn't build a car or a computer, or supply electric power. I couldn't play (let alone construct) a piano, though I might fashion a drum from a gourd and beat out a tune. I could scratch poems on something—a rocky ledge, perhaps—or recite them by a campfire. I could probably construct a shelter from branches. As a onetime Idaho farmboy I know how to ride a horse— if I could catch one. I could weave cloth from reeds. I could grow vegetables and build a fire to cook them—if I had matches, which I don't know how to make, or could use flint, which I don't know where to find. My point is this: the complex social order we take for granted depends upon a continuously creative human culture; and evil threatens to destroy it. The good news of Jesus is that evil—the gates of hell—cannot prevail against the heavenly good.

From this standpoint heaven is a God-given, eternal repository of goals providing coherent beauty to human experience. Culture infuses biological time and space with eternal meaning. Culture gives context to self and society. Whenever and wherever acknowledged with appreciation and faithful stewardship, culture becomes God's commonwealth on earth, a rich and beneficent tapestry woven by the warp and woof of time and space.

Is heaven, then, a reality in culture? A godly humanist would say yes, and might reason as follows:

Look back upon humanity spreading like a flood across the earth over recent millennia. View the creative cusp of cosmic development. Might not the myth of heaven constitute a tested symbol for how human beings are socialized by receiving rewards for activities that benefit the whole of society and that endure through time? Some powerful energy must have fueled this exponential spread of intelligence that, despite appalling violence and tragedy, has spawned a world civilization, has altered the planet earth considerably, and has now begun to conquer space.

In this view, heaven as ideal community constitutes a triggering mechanism for such remarkable phenomena. *Heaven* is the name people give a myth of godly force as significant as worship, as central as consciousness, as solid as culture. This myth provides moral boundaries for human aspirations essential to civilization. Within a heavenly framework, ethics, religion, and aesthetics become grounded in eternal ideas and not in the physical structures of the world. Meaning is imposed by culture upon the cosmos, not drawn from it. As a cultural artifact defining hope, this idea of heaven sustains human solidarity in the face of a silent and often hostile natural world. The metaphor of heaven offers humanity a useful social construct, a prototype for goal-setting, an incentive for maximizing results through mutual human endeavor. In defying death and entropy, culture in this view offers the last word. In triumph over raw nature, humanity gains eternal life.

The view that heaven is located in culture is expressed and questioned in the dialogue of this poem:

"WHO'S RIGHT, LORD?"

Lord, yesterday my neighbor and I discussed death.
A heart attack put him in a serious mood.
He's a retired professor and legislator.
His affluent children support art museums,
and his grandkids trek for green causes.
Mac says he's ready to bow out gracefully;
content to let his influence live on.
Claims it's the noble thing to do.
I don't buy this.
From what I learned in Sunday school
I figure on a more personal afterlife.
Besides, I don't have kids.
Who's right, Lord? [6]

PRAYERS AT TWILIGHT

Ah, but in Mac's vision lurks the question that won't go away: What happens to me when I die? Here again it is asserted that the noble person accepts death like a bunt softly laid down so another player can advance. *One's religious faith triumphs through sacrifice. I must give way so others can find their ways. The personal life continues genetically, from mind to mind, and by means of a culture bearing the imprint of lives that demonstrate moral purpose. Personal faith is rewarded by seeing (albeit from afar) the kingdoms of this world becoming the kingdom of God. Death will not have the last word. Isn't that the message of the crucified Christ? Goodness transcends evil. Light puts out darkness. Heaven is here and now.* In sum, this pattern of life eternal infuses the transitory world with a meaning greater than the sum of its parts.

If the idealism of this and the previous heaven location leaves one feeling socially dutiful but personally melancholy, the following perspectives offer greater assurance of self-conscious survival after death. The major religions of the world—Judaism, Christianity, Baha'i, Islam, Buddhism, Hinduism, Taoism—all hold beliefs in some form of personal immortality. The same goes for animistic religions. We consider three such views next.

LOCATION FOUR:
A COEXISTENT SPIRITUAL REALITY

In this view the reality of heaven is lodged in a parallel universe, a spiritual world coexisting with the natural one. It's a higher level of reality, however, offering an orderly answer to the entropy and disorder that characterize the natural world. Think about it: *Isn't reality more than stuff and things? Isn't it more than a collage of social ideals? Mightn't it be better to separate heaven more sharply from the world that science describes and we sense? God is spirit. Well, then, let spiritual reality be reached by faith rather than by reason. Free the notion of heaven from subservience to scientific language. Release it from bondage to culture. Human civilization routinely collapses into anarchy. Culture succumbs to disasters natural or otherwise. There have been dark ages before; they will come again. Who knows the final conclusion for this world? Collapse, probably. Posit instead a separate realm of spirit (or soul) opposed to this mute and degenerating material realm of body and brain. Reasoning, after all, is a function of the physical body's nervous system.*

This alternate realm is envisioned as accessible to human beings through spiritual knowledge rather than through sense perception. This approach obviates the loss and certain death inevitably found within the natural world, including its human culture. *Turn the tables: see the material world as illusion; spirit is reality. Don't idolize death by nice stories about genetic immortality. Don't wrap culture with a cloak of eternity. Eternal substance belongs to the soul and not the body. The body is finite and transitory. So is the physical universe. Let the body die; let the cosmos freeze or fry. Heaven is an eternal realm of soul. It has no beginning and no ending. The spiritual realm is a parallel universe, but it's the enduring one. The material world is but a mirage of the spiritual world.*

This view of soul immortality got a boost from ancient Greeks such as the philosopher Plato and the Jewish scholar Philo, both of whom portrayed immateriality as the true reality and hinted at a continuance of self-consciousness through souls, which upon death would join other nonmaterial entities, like angels (*daemons*). With variations, this view had other advocates from the classic "golden age," such as the Chinese scholar Mo Tzu, whose "Son of Heaven" depicted a spiritual realm that gave hierarchical order to earthly society.

In this view, one's death isn't a sacrifice one makes for genetic or cultural survival, but a shucking of bodily encumbrance. What is eternal isn't lost, and that includes the soul. Souls, thought these philosophic ancients, can be reborn over and over again, in various forms (depending upon their response to rationality). In its long journey, each soul can—if it responds properly—rise to wisdom. True learning, Plato insisted, is recollection of eternal virtues. It means recalling what is.

Viewing heaven as the abode of souls, not bodies, sounds attractive. Especially when it comes to logistics. No need to puzzle about where to put everyone, what a new body would look like, whether there's sex in heaven, whether other forms of life continue (horses, maybe, but not flies?), and how a God who is spirit can sit upon a throne.

This sort of immortality isn't what traditional Jews, Christians, Muslims, and other theists generally have believed, but its philosophy, particularly through Gnosticism, did influence their ideas about body and soul. Its "separate realm" perspective tended to denigrate the natural world in favor of the world of the mind or of the spirit. The immaterial seemed more real than the material. The dualism of this view is at variance with the Hebraic holistic view of the person central in biblical teaching. As a result of such a sharp division of soul and body, monasticism flourished as a spiritual discipline: the route to holiness became the way of negation—keep the body down; wear hair shirts if vows of celibacy and poverty aren't sufficient disciplines. In education such a separation led to affirming the autonomy of intellect over deed and, by implication, the superiority of "white-collar" over "blue-collar" work.

With the rise of modern science the church retreated from its biblical, holistic understanding of persons "created in the image of God." As noted above, they handed the body over to the scientists and focused on the soul. But in Platonic terms, "souls" are immortal, not something to be resurrected. This has led to confusion—people celebrating Easter in litanies and creeds affirming the "bodily resurrection" while denying it by limiting immortality to immaterial souls.

This "separate realm" view in effect denies the resurrection of the personal body. If the soul is eternal, there's nothing to be resurrected. There are other problems, too. It isn't clear what souls would do all day, let alone all eternity. A protracted Socratic dialogue might not appeal to everyone. Many folks would prefer a more earthy heaven—certainly not as materialistic and chauvinist as one popular Muslim version of paradise, which promises men pretty girls (*houri*), feasts, and beautiful horses,[7] but one that does offer sensory enhancement rather than diminishment in the after-life. Transmigration of souls, accordingly, is more congenial to Hindus than to Jews and Muslims and Christians. As Frederick Buechner says, "The idea of the immortality of the soul is based on the experience of humanity's indomitable spirit. The idea of the resurrection of the body is based on the experience of God's unspeakable love."[8]

Furthermore, acceptance of a coexistent and greatly superior spiritual reality can foster neglect of the physical world people live in. It doesn't always result in some well-defined Confucian social order. A kind of fatalism often ensues from such disdain for the physical, contradicting the strong biblical mandate to care for the earth because the creation is good. And who knows whether a "phantom" universe isn't just another kind of pie-in-the-sky mythology? One could argue that it discriminately sanctions the lucky elite with good karma, allowing them to exploit the lower classes and avoid the hard work of living together without war, the hard work of healing the injured and the sick, feeding the hungry, clothing the naked, cleaning up the Ganges (or the Columbia), and caring for the earth responsibly. Subtle and sophisticated, this "superior reality" view offers a more readily exploited escape mechanism than one that cynics or liberation theologians usually dredge up—namely, that a paradise offering mansions on streets of gold is a sop tossed to the masses.

The hope of a better eventual reincarnation can be exploitive. It doesn't offer the kind of redemptive justice envisioned in the scene before the throne of heaven, where goodness is rewarded and evil punished. It doesn't foster the fervent social responsibility to which people commit themselves as witnesses to God's king-dom on earth. It fails to perceive earth as God's chosen stage for the drama of redemption. It misses the central message of the incarnation: in Christ God is reconciling the world to himself, and has entrusted that message to his followers (see 2 Cor. 5:18–20). Christ's followers are most heavenly minded when they're busy on earth as agents of such reconciliation. At the annunciation to Mary an angelic choir sang, "Glory to God in the highest heaven, and *on earth peace* among those whom he favors!" (Luke 2:14).

LOCATION FIVE:
A REALITY IN THE MIND OF GOD

> *The blessed in heaven perceive creatures free*
> *from every creaturely image . . . in that one image*
> *which is God, and in which God knows and loves*
> *and wills himself and all things.*[9]

MEISTER ECKHART

> *When we die the book is finished,*
> *but it will not be destroyed.*
> *It remains for eternity*
> *in the mind of God.*[10]

CHARLES HARTSHORNE

According to this view, heaven is located in the all-encompassing mind of God. Unity with the Infinite has a strong appeal. It answers the yearning for knowing God, not just knowing *about* him, thus affirming evangelical experience. Union with God is the goal of mystics of all time, who consider such unity the word that overcomes death. God cannot allow anything to be lost. Didn't Jesus say, "Now he is God not of the dead, but of the living; for to him all of them are alive" (Luke 20:38)? In this view death may destroy the body, but personal consciousness will be held forever in the Divine.

One Christian variant aims to keep scientific and religious explanations separate, but congruent. It goes like this: The church is Christ's resurrected form, his body. This is the church *terrestrial*. Those who have died are the church *celestial*. Rather than trying to locate a celestial region somewhere, as traditionalists do, proponents of this view see the departed as continuing in the mind of God. Thoughts and deeds aren't lost; they contribute to the process of God.[11] Having this hope encourages a prayerful seeking of union with the Divine.

Humanly speaking, "who we were" lasts only a few generations after our death, perhaps in books or stories, or in picture albums and antique furniture handed down to great-grandchildren. But after a few generations most of us will have been forgotten. The furniture will have fallen apart or have been sold at auction by descendants who need funds more than they need mementos. I have a few memories of my grandmother and a few documented memories of generations further back. And I've visited ancestral places in Holland and Wales, including a house built in 1638. But who are these remote ancestors of mine that a zealous genealogist friend traced back to the tenth century? They're proper names—just letters on a page. So, humanly speaking, even on calendar time individuals cease to be remembered quite soon. These are truly "disappeared" persons.

Spiritually speaking, in this view—heaven in the all-encompassing mind of God—no one, however insignificant socially, will ever be unknown to God. Everything that has or increases value will be preserved for future generations, and even though human creatures eventually disappear from the cultural scene, God eternally remembers "who we were." He keeps the *Homo sapiens* family album. Our life record is archived in a divine repository. Good, bad, or indifferent, we remain forever in God's book of life. It's all there—no missing tapes, no hype or slander, no misrepresentation, no social oblivion. Nothing can wipe clean the slate of our existence. Our highest dreams and achievements, our loves and sacrifices, our quests for truth—everything we've been and done is preserved with God. So the lesson is that we should walk faithfully in this life—it's enough of a challenge—and not worry about the next. God will never forget us.

At best this view puts God on a high shelf. Accordingly, it may engender a worshipful attitude among religious seekers and foster spiritual discipline among dissatisfied secularists. God immanent has been stressed more than God transcendent during the past half-century; in fact, in many places of worship people are made to feel right chummy with the Divine. But does this view of eternity as lodged in the mind of God *really recover transcendence?*

For many moderns it does not. The high shelf is the forgotten one. Gone is terror before God's thundering voice; gone are shame and guilt at having offended Jehovah. Instead, it seems, Deo exists to massage ego. People used to shudder before the judge of all the earth. People used to weep for their sins at altars of prayers or in confessionals. Now people clap for prayer songs instead of prostrating themselves before the Lord. Aesthetics has replaced ethics; performance has replaced ministry. My own Christian ancestors and their friends were dubbed "Quakers" because they literally trembled in worship before the Lord. Now, alas, some inheritors of that tradition pick apart the Bible, equate God with *gaia* (or divinize nature), revel in religious process, and downgrade Jesus to an early social revolutionary.

While viewing heaven as resting in God's mind is no guarantee of recovered transcendence, a renewed mystical approach might recover *awe.* Mystics assert that divine ecstasy is the most overwhelming human experience possible (better than even the sex or power or money touted by TV culture). I'm not much of a contemplative, but a few times in my life God has overwhelmed me with a presence so awesome it's hard to describe. This has happened to others as well—some who put pen to paper and share the experience, and many more who are too intimidated by secular culture or at such a loss for words they wrap these experiences in a cloak of silence. My own conversion sixty-five years ago was an overwhelming event. And since then I've experienced a few powerful epiphanies. When the Lord floods me with awe and mystery, I resonate with Isaiah of old: "Woe is me! I am lost, for I am a man of unclean lips, and I live among a people of unclean lips; yet my eyes have seen the King, the LORD of hosts!" (Isa. 6:5).

At such times "Holy, holy, holy" is no longer just a hymn numbered 323 but rather a penitent paean of praise. The earth, indeed, is full of God's glory! So I have tasted the mystics' golden nectar. I have sampled the ecstatic union with the Divine that Eastern Orthodoxy proclaims as the highest form of spirituality. At such blissful times I know that God will never forsake me, no matter how dire the circumstances. The song "His faithful follower I would be, for by his hand He leadeth me" rings true! Such mountaintop experiences make it easier to slog it out in the valley, which, of course, is where we live most of the time. Many of life's valleys are hard to navigate. We tend to stumble in our trek through them. Ecstatic touches from God pull us through. Yes, they do!

So, this is a high view of an all-inclusive God, sovereign, never forgetting a sparrow that falls, forever reaching out to weld us unto himself. But this view of heaven puts quite a burden on us mortals. Somehow, it's hard for me to imagine an ecstatic moment lasting forever. Union with the Divine is okay, but I crave wiggle-room to be me. Please don't misunderstand. Like you, I should be more prayerful and contemplative. I should focus more on mystical meditation. Should pray for an hour instead of for five minutes. Mystical unity with God *is* an optimum quality for this life, but it doesn't quite satisfy active people of flesh and blood if it limits heaven to a glorified mind trip. Furthermore, how does such unity with the Divine *on a forever basis* differ from the "emptiness" of Nirvana? And what happens to *me* if I'm absorbed into the mind of the Divine?

Must my humanity be diminished for God's glory? (Like Job, I'm arguing with God now, though with fear and trembling.) We're God's creatures, and although we flub and sin, God continues to reach out to redeem and restore us. Such is the word of grace that Jesus taught. This atonement is what we celebrate in worship. We may be clay in the Potter's hands, but is that metaphor the whole story? No. We're fashioned *in the image of the Creator*. We're not just pure spirits for God to toy with and put in a heavenly closet at day's end. We're not just software for God's computer. Christ's agony in Gethsemane powerfully portrays God's proffered redemption. God's offer of love is laced with blood, sweat, and tears. It was sent to us through an agonizing death on a cruel imperial cross. God entered our condition, became flesh. Became one of us. Incarnate. How then can our discipleship, often costly, be limited to this life in the flesh? How can God's offer of redemption be temporary in personal experience and then just eternally stashed away in divine memory banks after our death?

Some mystics find absorption into the Absolute thrilling, but most of us would be disappointed if our purpose in life turned out to be making God look good. And if that were the case, the question would be: For whom? Is there an implied polytheism here (God bragging to other gods about his photo collection)? This view suffers by turning the living God into a mental idol called Pure Thought. I prefer a God who flings fire into darkness, who spins energy at light-speed into a hundred billion massive galaxies, who creates minerals, vegetables, and animals. Who shapes human beings out of dust and walks with them in the garden at sunset. Who dusts off his hands and calls the whole shebang good. I prefer the God of Abraham and Moses and Jesus, the God and father of us all. I prefer a God who bears our sins on a cross to demonstrate that he loves us bodily creatures. Who forgives penitent sinners such as David, Mary Magdalene, and the thief on the cross, and who forgives me. We worship a God who redeems fallen humanity and patiently waits to complete a cosmic creation process now impeded by sin. This is glory! So let's look for heaven in a location more agreeable to our hopes and more compelling to our minds—that is, when our hopes and minds are centered on the will and power of God.

LOCATION SIX: A REALITY CONGRUENT WITH CREATION

> *THERE is a land of pure delight*
> *Where saints immortal reign,*
> *Infinite day excludes the night,*
> *And pleasures banish pain.*
>
> *There everlasting Spring abides,*
> *And never-withering flowers:*
> *Death like a narrow sea divides*
> *This heav'nly land from ours.*[12]

ISAAC WATTS

In this view the reality of heaven is located within creation, of which the cosmos itself is the part now open to our (limited) understanding. To put it another way, heaven is the context for the world we experience through our ordinary senses.

Exploring heaven through the created world is difficult, because our minds aren't geared to its dimensions. But clues lie scattered about. Where are they? Look in history, in the human mind, in culture, in the revelations of God, and in the physical universe itself. This view finds intimations of heaven from God's word spoken in and through nature, history, the stories of humankind, and Scripture. Broadly, this is how heaven is envisioned by Jews, Muslims, Christians, and many other persons as well.

Christians find in the death of Jesus the procuring cause of human salvation—for all persons of all time. The Word of creation has become the Word of redemption. As the prologue to John's Gospel puts it, "The true light, which enlightens everyone, was coming into the world" (John 1:9). Christians also find the resurrection of Jesus to be the confirming sign of their own resurrection. In resurrecting Jesus, God answers our questions with a resounding "Yes!"

Those who hold this view have been somewhat reticent about affirming it publicly. This occurs partly because people are embarrassed by wild cultic speculations about heaven and by hype from religious entrepreneurs, and partly because they've been intimidated by science. *Wrongly* intimidated by science, in my judgment, for rightly understood, science is but an effort to read God's Word in creation. Bizarre and sadly tragic cultic efforts to "storm heaven's gates" are reminders that being too heavenly minded is of no earthly good. And that we ought not speculate beyond the boundaries God has set. Nevertheless, the witness to a realm of afterlife is persistent over time and within culture. Counterfeit bills don't discredit good currency; they testify to its value.

The universe is an enormous place (expanding at an accelerating rate) with vast, untapped mysteries. According to some scientists, ordinary matter makes up only five percent of cosmic reality, and we're in contact with only ten percent. How they measure a tenth of an unknown isn't clear to me, but I take their word for it that there's a lot to the cosmos we have neither eyes nor instruments to perceive, nor brainpower to fathom. Yet.

So, in this view, although heaven is mostly unexplored territory, there are clues that suggest it's as much a part of reality as cats and dogs, microbes and moose, whales and wrens, mountains and oceans, as real as people, as eternal as God. It's this reality that concepts delineate and culture shapes to human purpose. Heaven is as much a part of cosmic reality as suns and quarks and black holes and a hundred billion whirling galaxies. Actually, the term *heaven* signifies a divine driving force behind space/time reality. It embodies the foundation and goal for the cosmos. It names the context of reality.

This view of heaven accepts mystery but finds intimations of eternity sufficiently compelling to create confidence in the hope of heaven—as a mystery revealed. Christians who hold this view believe that Jesus' triumph over death is a harbinger of our own victory. Jesus is the pioneer, the first one through the mountain pass, as it were. This view doesn't discredit the improved quality of life which the light of Christ brings in this life, but considers rather that the presence of God's Spirit with us and within the community of faith is but earnest money on a heavenly home. Salvation may begin in life, but it continues beyond death. As Paul said, "If for this life only we have hoped in Christ, we are of all people most to be pitied" (1 Cor. 15:19). John Donne exclaimed in memorable verse, "Death be not proud, though some have called thee mighty and dreadful. . . . [O]ne short sleep past, we wake eternally, and death shall be no more; death, thou shalt die."[13] Death is not the last word. Life is the final word; and that life includes conscious personal continuation beyond the tunnel of death. Proponents of this view consider that it fulfills the other concepts of immortality, finding in them intimations of heaven made explicit through scriptural revelation, and particularly through the resurrection of Jesus Christ.

This is where I stand. I hold this view along with other persons of faith over the centuries. Heaven has continuity with the created order we now enjoy. Indeed, it is the alpha and the omega, the beginning and the end. We await a renewed heaven and earth marked by righteous character and offering increased dimensions for a fuller life.

In subsequent chapters we will explore heaven, looking at its evidence (its "maps"), checking out its inhabitants, and pondering personal changes, probable activities, social order, and cosmic renewal. But before commencing such exploration, it's important to examine a related concept: eternal life. For location one—heaven is nowhere—the adjective *eternal* is only a euphemism for enduring ideals. It has significance, however, for the other five views about heaven, especially those for whom the term signifies more than quality of life. The sixth is for me the most credible option for heaven's location: a reality congruent with creation. It conveys a spatial connotation, coherent with the term "eternal life," which correlates place with time. And most importantly, this location signifies that in the afterlife people will be *truly present in bodily form.*

THREE

What Does *"Eternal* Life" Mean?

As all things are produced through the Word eternally
spoken, so all things are restored, advanced and
completed through the Word united to flesh.[1]
—*Bonaventure*

"Perfect love casts out fear."
It is not by thinking ourselves right that we cease to fear.
It is simply by loving, and abandoning ourselves
to him whom we love without returning to self.
That is what makes death sweet and precious.
When we are dead to ourselves, the death of the body
is only the consummation of the work of grace.[2]
—*Francois Fénelon*

To consider that after the death of the body the spirit
perishes is like imagining that a bird in a cage will be
destroyed if the cage is broken, though the bird has
nothing to fear from the destruction of the cage.[3]
—*Abdu'l Baha*

In this chapter we examine what the term "eternal life" signifies, how eternal life is gained, and what sorts of transitions enable sinful people to stand perfected before the throne of a holy God. A listing of major biblical verses about eternal life appears in Appendix A.

WHAT DOES THE TERM *ETERNAL* MEAN?

Our ideas about heaven are shaped by our understanding of what it means for something to be eternal. I concluded the previous chapter by noting how the concept of "heaven" conveys a spatial connotation, whereas "eternal life" correlates place with time. It does this quantitatively and qualitatively. Consider two familiar biblical phrases. Psalm 23 (KJV): "Surely goodness and mercy shall follow me all the days of my life: and I will dwell in the house of the LORD for ever." And from John 3:16 (KJV): "For God so loved the world, that he gave his only begotten Son, that whosoever believeth in him should not perish, but have everlasting life."

Generally speaking, by "eternal life" people imply two meanings, sometimes but not always commingled. The first sense indicates that individuals continue to exist in an *everlasting* way, continuously. This conveys quantitative significance. Hebrew poetry often puts the words *eternal* and *everlasting* in parallel equivalency—e.g., "eternal mountains" and "everlasting hills" (Hab. 3:6). The word *eternal* and synonyms such as *forever* and *always* denote duration over time. Used in this way *eternity* portrays the arrow of time as measured by clocks and calendars, as seconds, minutes, days, months, years, centuries, eras, ages, millennia, aeons. In this sense *eternal* means that the arrow of time penetrates the wall of death and continues indefinitely, forever. Time indicates beings acting sequentially within the boundaries of material and spatial limits. Eternity *encompasses* time as one of its dimensions.

In a second sense the term *eternal* denotes a quality of life not subject to passing time. John 17:3 is a biblical example of this sense: "This is eternal life: that they may know you, the only true God, and Jesus Christ, whom you have sent." Used this way, "eternal life" connotes character values such as love, loyalty, friendship, steadfastness, fidelity, and veracity. Collectively, qualities of good character are often termed "eternal verities." They persist in all temporal circumstances. Biblical scholarship generally holds that for early Christians the term "eternal life" combines the strong Hebrew sense of an historical, temporal process with Platonic notions of a superior, nonmaterial, timeless world.[4]

We look now at how eternal life is variously perceived, at what continues after death or is immune from it. In doing so we discover how "after" sometimes signifies a sequence of events, a *following* after death, and how it sometimes signifies an impingement upon time, a nontemporal *alternative* to death. This, then, is a key question: How does eternity encompass quality and quantity—that is, quality of life and continuance of life? How does eternity conjoin past and future within an eternal present?

NATURALISTIC, CULTURAL, AND RELIGIOUS PERSPECTIVES ON ETERNAL LIFE

The wide range of perspectives on eternal life can be divided into three main categories: naturalistic, cultural, and religious. Let's look at some of the many differing understandings of eternal life that fall within these categories.

From a *naturalistic* point of view eternal life reflects one or more of the following concepts:

- Continuing evolution, with its enduring genetic repository arising from natural selection—a repository to be guarded by intelligent beings against losses, even within lesser species.

- An environmental cycle drawing energy from light in a rhythmic pattern of post-death decay that fertilizes new growth in flora and eventually in fauna, thus nurturing continuous life. (In this view *nature* is immortal.)
- A reincarnation of lifeforms as intelligence embedded in tissue surfaces along an evolutionary biological scale, rising to new heights through intelligent and purposive reconstruction.

From a *cultural* point of view eternal life means one or more of the following concepts:

- Residual artifacts that endure over time—languages of all sorts, public and residential structures, agricultural practices, arts and crafts, inventions, roads and transportation, modes of understanding, mathematical formulae, recipes, memorabilia, history, sagas, fiction, poetry, music, religions, museums, parks, statuary, technical skills, designs, and machinery. Once brought into existence by human creativity, these artifacts continue indefinitely, becoming part of a universe of discourse knitting into coherence material and energy, and offering modes of social interaction.
- Memory repositories in the minds and albums of family and friends, or preserved in documents, or related orally from one generation to the next, enriching posterity forever.
- The ubiquitous enrichment of the community of selves through language, customs, mores, and codes expressing ethical, religious, and aesthetic values and useful norms of

conduct. This enrichment may come through wisdom for living deposited laterally (qualitatively) along the arrow of time in patterns of value for family, labor, and community behavior, or it may come through knowledge spreading incrementally through human consciousness and its accessory tools and repositories of language, culture, social structure, machinery, and artificial intelligence.

- The political power of the empire as the sustainer of human values through time and space. In the classic Roman era a phrase used for the emperor, *pontifex maximus*—"highest bridge to God"—signified empire as *the* divine agency for human society, defending civilization against dark forces of parochialism and anarchy, and overcoming the hostility of nature. (Early Christians went to their death for refusing to worship Caesar; they found in Jesus Christ not empire, but the bridge to God's kingdom.)

From a *religious* point of view eternal life includes one or more of the following concepts:

- Reincarnation (or the transmigration of souls) in cycles of animate forms, lower and higher, endlessly progressing toward, or degenerating from, personhood.
- A substratum of spirituality beneath the illusion or limitation of material substance and temporality.
- The infusion of glory and goodness into temporal life. This perspective, more consistent with monotheism than the previous views, brings a timeless dimension to whatever goodness triumphs over inevitable bodily death.
- The return of individual self-consciousness to collective consciousness—that is, a fusing of one's identity with a nonembodied Godhead.

- The return of a person's soul to God, although the body decays.
- A church that, as the body of Christ, transcends death. The church achieves that transcendence by offering a continuing divine presence in a community of persons being renewed in righteousness, and by celebrating God's redemptive process via worship, witness, and service to humanity.
- Personal reembodiment after death, with retention of identity, personality, and accreted memories, and with capacities enhanced and freed for creative and everlasting activity in a renewed cosmos.

AN ENCOMPASSING UNDERSTANDING OF THE ETERNAL

The last two religious viewpoints convey the meaning of eternal life most fully to me. They combine qualitative and quantitative meanings, affirming and correlating *both* creation and redemption. They provide a context for incorporating complex and magnificent naturalistic processes as well as beautiful cultural aspirations and artistic dreams. As an active participant in the church visible, I find myself already experiencing the eternal in worship, fellowship, and service. I also experience the eternal in nature (watching the waves crash over tide pools, for example) and in cultural interaction (sharing scones with neighbors at a bakery on Saturday mornings, or painting a word picture into a tribute to a friend).

Not a single sparrow falls to the ground, said Jesus, without God's knowledge, making the point that human beings, more valuable than many sparrows, shouldn't fear: God loves and cares for them, too (Matt. 10:29–30). Sparrows aren't particularly significant culturally; they're not pets like dogs. Even birders don't travel miles to see the common sparrow. The sparrow isn't any country's national bird, nor is it depicted on coins. No athletic team is known as the "Mighty Sparrows."[5]

My point is that eternal life impacts the whole of creation. If sparrow society is valuable, then how much more are work crews and family vacations, romances and city councils, ball games and musical performances. Whatever is good has eternal value. God's kingdom is within and among us in the love we share, in the justice we seek, and in the culture that surrounds us—a culture enriched by scientific inquiry and artistic creation. Qualities endure—such is God's promise to us. This present experience of a timeless eternity is but a prelude to an exponentially greater experience, one that transcends death. The eternal verities we now enjoy point to a reality beyond this life, beyond the present configuration of the cosmos, when more fully than now we will "dwell in the house of the Lord forever."

The bodily resurrection of Jesus supports a view of eternity that provides duration for natural and cultural values. Ian Barbour, one of several modern scholars who are bridging the unfortunate chasm between science and religion, affirms a unitary view of the self. He writes:

> In sum, it would be consistent with both the scientific and the biblical outlook to understand the person as a *multileveled unity* who is both a biological organism and a responsible self. We can escape both dualism and materialism if we assume a holistic view of persons with a hierarchy of levels. Some of these levels we share with all matter, some we share with all living things, some with all animal life, while some seem to be uniquely human. . . . In the biblical view, it is this integral being whose whole life is of concern to God.[6]

This biblical view contrasts with Platonic and other philosophical idealisms in which the soul exists without beginning and ending, outside of time. It contrasts with religious views that deprecate bodily existence and define salvation as deliverance from all temporality and materiality. That eternal life signifies continuing bodily existence is a doctrine shared by Jewish, Christian, and Muslim theologies. About belief in the resurrection, Rabbi Alan L. Ponn notes, "Today it is accepted in all Jewish denominations, except that the Reform Jews assert that there will be only a resurrection of the soul."[7]

A strong belief in an eternal afterlife spawned the church as a witness to the significance of Jesus, God's incarnate Word, making explicit the intimations of eternal life within earlier Scriptures. It accounted for Christianity's rapid growth. This sentence from an early historian, Luke, indicates the key to that growth: "With great power the apostles gave their testimony to the resurrection of the Lord Jesus, and great grace was upon them all" (Acts 4:33).

The Gospel accounts show that the first followers of Jesus were initially baffled by the empty tomb, but they became convinced, after Jesus' appearances to them, that he had indeed risen. Not resuscitated, but resurrected into a new body moving through space and time differently than before but somehow similarly. Early believers struggled to interpret this example of continuity in tension with discontinuity in the order of things. The record of the early church reveals that this belief met resistance from one Jewish party, the Sadducees, "[which authorities were] . . . much annoyed because they were teaching the people and proclaiming that in Jesus there is the resurrection of the dead" (Acts 4:2).

The record shows also that a converted leader of the Pharisee party (which did believe in resurrection), Paul of Tarsus, to whom the risen Lord appeared in a special epiphany, challenged the unbelief of the intellectual Greek community. Here is the account of one such confrontation:

. . . [S]ome Epicurean and Stoic philosophers debated with him. Some said, "What does this babbler want to say?" Others said, "He seems to be a proclaimer of foreign divinities." (This was because he was telling the good news about Jesus and the resurrection.) . . . When they heard of the resurrection of the dead, some scoffed; but others said, "We will hear you again about this." (Acts 17:18, 32)

We know that many people wanted to hear more about the resurrection from Paul, and from the others to whom the Word of the Lord had come. For Christianity has spread around the world, and continues to spread, reaching diverse groups in all sorts of cultures, testifying to the good news of God's offer of redemption from sin and of life eternal. Why such transcultural reception of Christianity? One basic reason is that the Gospel affirms the yearnings and the hopes for eternal life that God has planted in every human heart.

HOW IS ETERNAL LIFE GAINED?

Who gains eternal life in heaven (rather than enduring the torments of hell), and by what process of salvation, isn't the main focus of this book, but it's an important question, so in response I offer a central Christian principle about salvation (with several metaphors elaborating that principle), along with five major biblical teachings that provide context. The central principle is that through Christ's death and resurrection God brings salvation to humanity. Through this central historical event of *atonement*, God graciously—that is, by *grace*—expiates sin and brings sinners to righteousness. That we're saved by *grace* doesn't mean the absence of human will; it means, rather, that God's help is totally needed and freely offered.

How does Jesus' death bring us to righteousness? Here are four historic answers and one contemporary one.

- *Christ ransoms us from the devil.* This social metaphor is more apt than we care to acknowledge. Think about hostages who are taken for money or political ends, pawns for whom ransom cannot be paid lest more hostages get taken; or ponder rulers who must pay off drug dealers to get their children back.

    This theory of atonement pictures people trapped by evils from which Christ rescues them. Early Christians referred to Jesus as the price God paid Satan to release them (and us) as hostages. Jesus was put in hell's stockade for our freedom. But hell couldn't hold him, as the resurrection demonstrates. Jesus gave his life as a "ransom for many" is how two biblical writers phrased it (Mark 10:45; 1 Tim. 2:6). Sin is conquered, evil defeated.

    We rejoice whenever God delivers the poor from economic bondage or offers the homeless a habitat, using human instruments for these purposes. We rejoice when God sets prisoners of all kinds free, including persons imprisoned by addictions of any kind, including addictions to drugs, gambling, lust, greed, egotism, hate, and (fundamentally) pride.

    People delivered from traps of their own setting or from those set by others don't quibble about modes of deliverance. "Free at last!" That's what ransomed people sing.

- *Christ satisfies the honor of the divine.* Nearly a thousand years ago an English theologian wrote a pamphlet titled "Why Did God Become Man?" Anselm used the metaphor of royalty insulted to explain atonement. He reasoned thus: a ruler may wish to forgive an insult, but the state's honor is at stake, so he can't. By this analogy sin so grossly insults God that it requires more than humanity can muster to satisfy the offense. Accordingly, God accepts the sacrificial death of Jesus, who as a *human* (one of us) takes the rap representatively, and as *God* satisfies the insult. Thus God's honor is preserved and divine love demonstrated.

Does this make God look petty? Not if you keep in mind that metaphors point to realities beyond themselves, not to exact equivalence. Look at human experience: sin is an enormous affront to the universe God created! Ponder the social insults that sustain this picture—jousts between jilted lords, duels, tribal gunfights. In the old city of Prague, in 1618, a group of Protestant nobles threw a Hapsburg prince from a window. The noble wasn't hurt—a circumstance Catholics attributed to angels and Protestants to luck in landing on a haystack—but the insult nonetheless precipitated a war that lasted thirty years. We don't have to look far to see more recent cycles of ethnic insult and retaliation, do we? Think of Ireland, Palestine, Burundi, and more.

And we can see societal insults much closer to home: ponder the insult to humanity when a parent drops a child over a cliff or boys murder a toddler for fun, when a serial rapist chops up victims, or when financial schemers con retirees out of life savings. The *public,* as well as the family, is outraged. Like Abel's blood, such insults cry from the ground for retribution. Such acts insult humanity made in the image of God. They insult God.

On the cross God's honor is affirmed, *and so is humanity's.* Sin is condemned and righteousness affirmed. God satisfies the insult of sin in ways both just and loving. Jesus' death suffices. God's honor is satisfied, and so is ours.

- *Christ substitutes for us.* According to this theory of the atonement, Christ takes the punishment we deserve. He bears the curse laid on us for having broken principles that in our mind we accept. This view isn't about paying extortion money to the devil or salvaging divine honor, but about breaking divine law. Again, the point isn't to equate God with a harsh judge, but to show the significance of Jesus' crucifixion. Persons of conscience, having with shame and sorrow acknowledged sin, may be instructed in the meaning of Christ's death for them.

  When seventeenth-century reformer George Fox languished in jail because of his quest for religious freedom, a young friend offered to take his place. England's leader, Oliver Cromwell, hearing of this offer, asked his councillors, "Which of you would do the same for me?" No one volunteered. When God asked who would take the rap for the worst of us, Jesus replied, "I will." Of his own choice he bore our punishment, even to death.

  The substitutionary view shows Christ empathizing with humanity. Jesus is tempted just as we are, yet without sin. In Gethsemane he sweats out his fears of what happens to good people in a bad world. He is one of us, and by his stripes we are healed. A person who comes to the aid of a broke or errant brother or sister receives more than cheery thanks. Bonding occurs between benefactor and benefited. Recipients of grace follow Christ as Lord by taking up the cross. They, too, demonstrate substitutionary love.

- *Christ is a moral influence.* A fourth way to explain how Christ's death procures human righteousness is the "moral influence" theory. As stated by a twelfth-century monk, Peter Abelard, the theory goes like this:

For grace to be really free and unmerited, a loving God must bear the burden of human sin without attaching conditions, such as having to pay off the devil, assuage insults, or exact fines for breaking divine law. God's unconditional love is so powerfully revealed in the life and death of Jesus that it awakens within sinners a reciprocal response. "We love him because he first loved us." This metaphor also draws upon social experience. A smile earns a smile; those who treat others respectfully receive reciprocal respect.

This theory raises questions, however. How can Jesus' death effect moral transformation if it depends on our attitudes? Can people just dispassionately decide for good or evil? If they're that morally free, what difference does Jesus' death make? Carnality seems insufficiently acknowledged. Another objection is that the theory situates Jesus in series with other influential charismatic martyrs.

Despite these problems there's merit in the view. What more powerfully motivates than unconditional love? Why should love be demeaned as causally insufficient to account for God's transformation of human character?—especially when one recognizes that the church is Christ's body. The one in whose name we conclude our prayers is not my Lord only and Lord of the church, but also Lord of history and Lord of the cosmos. Love is energy, and suffering love supremely so. The writer of Hebrews says: "It was fitting that God, for whom and through whom all things exist, in bringing many children to glory, should make the pioneer of their salvation perfect through suffering" (Heb. 2:10–11).

- *Christ is the peacemaker.* George Fox University professor Phil Smith adds to these historic theories a contemporary picture of the atonement: Christ as peacemaker.[8] He delineates it thus: "God appears again as the righteous king, and the human race as rebels against his legitimate rule. . . . God fights to win the rebels in the most surprising way, by becoming the defenseless Lamb of God." Professor Smith finds scriptural support from the conflict imagery of Revelation, from Jesus' parable about tenants conspiring to kill the heir and claim the inheritance (Mark 12:6–8), and from Paul's metaphor of rebels reconciled through Jesus' death: "Since we have now been justified in his blood, how much more shall we be saved from God's wrath through him! For if, when we were God's enemies, we were reconciled to him through the death of his Son, how much more, having been reconciled, shall we be saved through his life! Not only is this so, but we also rejoice in God through our Lord Jesus Christ, through whom we have now received reconciliation" (Rom. 5:9–11, NIV).

We will never remove mystery from the atonement. But the metaphors outlined above help our minds understand how Jesus' death brings salvation. The *ransom theory* of atonement shows salvation as release from sin's snares. The *satisfaction theory* pictures Jesus as conservator of bankrupt humanity. The *substitutionary theory* shows the cross regenerating human goodness. The *moral influence theory* highlights the power of God's unconditional love. The *peacemaker theory* shows how God's power reconciles rebellious humanity. The atonement may not be easily explained, even with the help of these metaphors, but it can be experienced without difficulty. To this I witness with profound joy!

We turn now to five major biblical teachings that give context for the principle that eternal life is procured through the atoning death of Jesus Christ.

First, God is the final judge of human actions and intentions. As the apostle Peter put it, "God shows no partiality, but in every nation anyone who fears him and does what is right is acceptable to him" (Acts 10:34–35). Peter's affirmation should ease our minds: we're not on the selection committee to determine who gains heaven and who doesn't, and neither are other folks! Furthermore, eternal life provides divine redress for inequities on earth that arise from ignorance and especially from sin. Human judgments are fallible and often biased; consequently, innumerable victims cry out for a redress of wrongs that only God can provide. People can be falsely accused by the court of public opinion as well as by the judiciary. Penitent sinners find God more forgiving than their social peers, from whom they may bear a lifelong stigma of moral failure.

Violence embedded in cycles of tyranny and anarchy, and fostered by depraved culture, has provided a pattern for society. This pattern will end. The throne of God is the final and determinative court of appeal, to which all are brought—rich or poor, favored or scorned, innocent or guilty. The biblical pictures of God holding court on a golden throne, and the popular image of Peter checking tickets at the pearly gate, symbolize a powerful check against usurpation of divine sovereignty by human institutions, whether by persons, clans, tribes, states, cliques, pressure groups, or corporations. Retributive justice is owed many persons, and God won't let them down. One doesn't have to read far in the Scriptures to understand that vengeance belongs to the Lord. Right will prevail, not wrong. Heaven reflects divine judgment.

Second, the light from God that illumines each conscience has been outwardly manifested in Jesus Christ. Incarnation signifies the embodiment of God's saving Word. The prologue to John's Gospel puts it succinctly: "The Word became flesh and lived among us." God's light shines within each person's conscience to impart knowledge of right and wrong. People can penitently accept and obediently follow that light, or they can reject it, sear their conscience, and become alienated from God—forever, if they wish. As one of Jesus' best-known sayings puts it, "For God so loved the world that he gave his only Son, so that everyone who believes in him may not perish but may have eternal life" (John 3:16).

The apostle Peter understood God's compassion. He wrote, "The Lord . . . is patient with you, not wanting any to perish, but all to come to repentance" (2 Pet. 3:9). The apostle Paul, a self-acknowledged zealot for God's covenant with Israel, was forced by the risen Christ to realize that salvation was available to others than his ethnic group. In dialogue with Athenian philosophers he commented on seeing in the city an idol to an unknown god. Paul said that what they worshiped as unknown he proclaimed as God. He asserted that God is close by and can be found by all who search, or even grope, for him (Acts 17:22ff).

As noted above, Christians hold the death and resurrection of Jesus to be the procuring cause for human salvation—for persons anywhere, anytime, of whatever culture, ignorant or learned. Beneficiaries of God's grace aren't limited to persons who've heard the "good news" verbally preached, although obviously it helps greatly for people to know that the deepest intimations of their hearts are confirmed by God's Word historically revealed in Jesus Christ.

Hearing the Gospel story amplifies the divine light in the conscience. Persons heeding the Gospel are freed from fears of a capricious or cruel deity and delivered from exploitive priestcraft. That's why missionaries have been so much appreciated by persons in animistic societies. The "good news" is gladly received by widely diverse groups. In Christ, indeed, there is no east and west, no north and south. Despite being fallible and sometimes ignorant of cultural nuances, these messengers of God have amplified human awareness of God's grace and of God's power over evil. Whatever the strength of that inward light, God judges all of us by the true intent of the heart, by our faithful response. All prayerful yearnings reach God's ear. The words people use to describe God's saving response to their cries from the heart are secondary to the light of God experienced and its saving force affirmed. Christ is, indeed, the "light of the world."

Third, we don't earn heaven. Salvation is by God's grace, through faith. In other words, it's a gift. Accordingly, no one has bragging rights. Odious comparisons are out. No priestly office, no ritual, no temple blessing, no social status controls admission or confers special privileges in heaven. Jesus rebuked his disciples for trying to cinch executive appointments in the coming kingdom. Heaven is a gift to all persons who penitently exclaim, as did the old prophet Isaiah (dazzled by a vision of God's splendor), "Woe is me, for I am lost!" (Isa. 6:5), or who cry out, as did a contrite public servant confronted with God's holiness in the ministry of Jesus, "God, be merciful to me, a sinner!" (Luke 18:13). These are the sort of people fit for heaven.

God's gracious redemption is spelled out in the "good news" of the life, death, and resurrection of Jesus. Heaven completes the salvation begun in this life. Spiritual discipline on earth schools us for eternal life. This doesn't mean that we enter heaven equally mature, however. Greater responsibilities in heaven will accrue to those who have demonstrated greater spiritual preparation on earth. This reward for faithfulness is hinted at in one of Jesus' parables: "Because you have been trustworthy in a very small matter, take charge of ten cities" (Luke 19:17). Still, entrance to heaven is by *faith,* not by *works.* Jesus' parable about laborers hired at late hours of the day, and for full pay, reinforces that dictum.

Fourth, through the incarnation God has validated the creation. God "becoming flesh" affirms the worth and dignity of physical existence, including the dignity of physical bodies. People are part of nature. Contrary to what is implied by some eco-terrorists, we human beings belong here. Indeed, the Genesis account relates that God pronounced each step of creation "good" and the creation of humanity "very good." So heaven is for real, whole persons, and not just a divine harvesting of their ideas or their memories or their genes. No stripping them bare of bodies to extract souls, but rather a glorification of their persons with spiritual bodies. No diminishment of the earth that has nurtured and sustained them, but its enhancement within the cosmos. Heaven is fulfilled in God's cosmic re-creation.

Fifth, heaven is for redeemed people. The Bible is full of references about people being *cleansed* from sin, not just *forgiven* their sin. One biblical symbol of such cleansing is the wearing of white robes. It signifies that *ordinary* people achieve high status, not just an elite few. In heaven the poorest peon sports a toga. Another symbol, difficult for modern persons to relate to but meaningful to those schooled in sacrificial religions, is that saints are ones who are "washed in the blood of the Lamb." Holiness comes at a high cost—God's cost as well as ours. Holiness is our calling and destiny. "Pursue peace with everyone, and the holiness without which no one will see the Lord" (Heb. 12:14). Redemption, we may conclude, transforms the social order as well as the individual.

WHAT ABOUT HELL?

Yes, what about hell? It isn't the topic of this book, but a few thoughts are appropriate here nonetheless. Hell is a merciful God letting folks have their own way when they refuse his. "To choose evil is to choose misery," states Jerry L. Walls, a Wesleyan scholar at Asbury Seminary, "and the one who so chooses does so freely."[9] Medieval Christian and Muslim scenarios of sinners standing at the final judgment in abject terror, "up to their ankles, their waists, their shoulders in sweat," as they await an eternal sentencing,[10] seem a bit much! Descriptions of hell as terrible fiery torment make a point, however, that a succession of anguished victims over millennia can relate to. Call to mind certain really awful people in history or in your experience. Wouldn't you suppose tortured victims and their families might feel vindicated by this sort of divine vengeance?

Divine wrath is an aspect of God's holiness. The Bible symbolizes hell as a "lake of fire" (Rev. 19:20). God will bring judgment upon evil perpetrators of horrendous crimes. Hell isn't only for sadists who hack people to bits or rape children, or for tyrants who command the mowing down of innocent people with machine guns, or for zealots who bomb themselves and others to shreds, or for venal officials who leave untried persons to rot in stinking jails. Hell accommodates those who willfully defy God's rule, spurn proffered grace, refuse God's judgment, and persist in going their own sinful way. In the language of the Koran, "Evil is an abode of the proud."[11]

And yet hell reveals a mercy far beyond any human cry for vengeance. Eternal life is offered even for those who shun God, reject God, hate God, disbelieve in God. A contemporary philosopher, Stephen T. Davis, considers hell "an expression not only of divine justice but of divine love."[12] These finally impenitent ones will live on forever in a realm reserved for them, in a society unleavened by the righteousness they profited from on earth but rejected for themselves. Such chaos is punishment enough. And because whenever and wherever sin reigns in life is a taste of hell, people know what it is they're choosing.

While hell is logically the proper home for unrepentant mass murderers, it will also include some outwardly nice people—those who in their arrogant minds and disobedient hearts defy God and despise others. In *The Great Divorce*, C. S. Lewis brilliantly illustrates the self-delusion of persons who have rejected God in one way or another, and focuses particularly upon how intellectual pride leads to apostasy. He depicts hell as a place of eternal bickering by self-centered people who can't stand their neighbors and who restlessly move often and far away. They won't relocate to heaven when offered (a bus runs daily), because, as Lewis explains in an apt metaphor, "The grass hurts their feet."[13] Perhaps the ultimate sin is that of Luciferian, enlightened people trying to upstage God.

Some people believe that God's love will/must wear away such resistance and eventually empty the place—burn away the dross, as it were. Others opine that a loving God will annihilate the resolutely impenitent rather than let them soak in misery forever. A leading Evangelical scholar, Clark Pinnock, believes that hell will result in termination, not endless misery. This seems to him a better alternative to endless bliss in heaven than a universalism which otherwise would seem to be implied by the character of God.[14] Some see mercy in termination for the damned, like putting a suffering pet to sleep. It's possible, but the Scriptures are silent about such scenarios. Consider the matter of divine consistency. Love doesn't coerce. Freedom is a great but terrible gift, which God risks in offering, and which we risk in using. But who would want the alternative? To be programmed robots? Surely not!

In contrast, heaven will surely be home for some outwardly unlikely folk whose uncouth manners on earth offend the aesthetic sensibilities of more cultured people, but whose hearts are right and who love God and their neighbors as themselves. We tend to judge persons by outward appearances, but God judges the intent of the heart and honors deeds flowing accountably from such goodwill. The criterion isn't social status but fearing God and doing what's right. As "gatekeeper" Peter said, "If you invoke as Father the one who judges all people impartially according to their deeds, live in reverent fear during the time of your exile" (1 Pet. 1:17).

WHAT TRANSITIONS ARE NEEDED IN ORDER TO STAND BEFORE GOD'S THRONE?

Heaven confronts us with the holiness of God. How are forgiven sinners purged of the sin-nature that has beset humanity since the Fall? Let's consider a few points of salvation doctrine pertinent to preparation for heaven. First, let's put to rest the beguiling notion that God is an indulgent grandparent who just takes us all in willy-nilly, or an ineffective sovereign powerless to halt continuing consequences of freedom built into his realm. Such smug, self-serving attitudes lack reverence before a holy God.

To stand before the throne of God at the judgment, when the book of life is opened, is scary to contemplate, if we're truly honest with ourselves. When we're truly penitent we're more likely to identify with the publican in Jesus' parable who prayed "God be merciful to me, a sinner," than to congratulate ourselves unctuously like a Pharisee on being the moral superior to this groveling sinner nearby. Theologians throughout the centuries have pondered how persons can make a proper transition into heaven, how they can become perfected in faith, how they can be made holy. The need for some sort of holding venue for heavenly immigrants gains force for us when we ponder honestly the enormity of evil in the world, and our own complicity (in varying degrees) in that evil.

Let's look at some scriptural texts that ground God's call to holiness and then consider different views about how God prepares us for eternal life. "Be perfect, as my heavenly father is perfect," said Jesus (Matt. 5:48). That's pretty straightforward, isn't it? And very challenging! No wonder the church has sometimes interposed forms of priestcraft to dilute the strength of Jesus' words. On many occasions, as noted in the Gospels, Jesus illustrated that call for holiness. For example he extolled justice, mercy, and penitent prayer rather than ritual purity, formal worship, and pretentious altruism. He admonished us to forgive not just our friends but also our enemies, to consider lust as sinful as adultery, to return good for evil. He modeled obedience to God by accepting crucifixion rather than yielding to political or ecclesial expediency.

The contrast between existence sullied by endemic sin and life freed from humanity's curse is expressed tersely by the apostle Paul: "As in Adam all die, so in Christ all will be made alive" (1 Cor. 15:22ff, NIV). The author of the book of Hebrews describes the goal of outward moral righteousness and inward heart-purity thus: "Pursue peace with everyone, and the holiness without which no one will see the Lord" (Heb. 12:14). In his letter to the Romans, Paul notes the good-evil conflict within each of us and explains why the Gospel is good news: "The law of the spirit of life in Christ Jesus has set you free from the law of sin and death" (Rom. 8:2; see also chaps. 7 and 8). Theologians argue what being "set free" means—whether (and to what extent) righteousness is imputed (that is, stamped okay by virtue of Jesus' saving death) or imparted (empowered by Christ's spirit) to us *in this life.* But they generally agree that in heaven it means both.

Given the biblical teaching, when and how does this perfecting occur? It occurs in this life; eternal life begins here and now. As Peter Kreeft says, "Earth is heaven's womb."[15] God's kingdom *is* among and within us. To this the church gives witness. The theological term for our earthly preparation is *justification,* which includes not only divine forgiveness of sins but also purification by the Holy Spirit from the sin-nature. In the book of Acts, Luke narrates how believers were baptized by the Holy Spirit and empowered to witness the good news to the ends of the earth.

But is such sanctification sufficient, or is something more required before admission to heaven? Historically, theologians have suggested that something more may be anticipated—in other words, that an interim or transitional state is required to prepare people for eternal life. Doctrines of *purgation,* as such perspectives are called, assume three things. First, that there will be an interim time before the final judgment (see 1 Thess. 4:13); second, that most persons enter heaven with lots of worldly baggage to unload at the gate and hence need help overcoming a moral or spiritual shortfall; and third, that God will do whatever is needed on behalf of persons whose hearts are right.

Views of the interim state include the following:

- A state of limbo
- A punitive purgatory
- Final sanctification at death
- Complete earthly sanctification
  (thus no transitional state needed)
- Hell as ultimate purgation
- Purgatory as preparation

Limbo. Within the Islamic tradition limbo is for "persons whose good deeds keep them from the Fire and whose evil deeds keep them from the Garden." Such persons are the last to enter heaven.[16] Limbo within the Roman Catholic tradition provides a transitional state within which infants who die unbaptized and innocent of guilt and people of faith prior to or outside the Christian orbit can be cleansed from the stain of original sin. (This presupposes the efficacy of water baptism to remit original sin but not remove its finite consequences.) Some theologians continue to hold that a degree of punishment is needed even for such persons. For others the teaching has become marginal at best, and is itself in limbo!

Purgatory as punishment. One might picture traditional Roman Catholic notions of purgatory as a sort of celestial woodshed where naughty but promising students are spanked as a corrective discipline. The Lord chastens those whom he loves in *this* life— why not the next? More formally, purgatory is understood as an interim during which unforgiven guilt is expiated and punishment meted out for sins committed even though forgiven. Although penitent sinners stand before God as baptized persons in a state of grace, purgatorial fires (*symbolic* fires, the Eastern church insisted) burn away their dross, bringing them to perfection. The great medieval Catholic theologian Thomas Aquinas cites approvingly from St. Augustine: "Even as in the same fire gold glistens and straw smokes, so in the same fire the sinner burns and the elect is cleansed."[17] Medieval tradition believed that certain really meritorious saints could skip purgatory—they had more goodness than they needed—making extra credits available to "spiritually challenged" folks.

This view of purgatory lost credibility when medieval promoters exploited the teaching as a money-raising gimmick for new cathedrals. Pay an indulgence and you could shorten a loved one's purgatorial sentence by drawing on church-banked surplus goodness. One little advertising jingle went something like this: "As soon as the coin in the coffer rings, a soul from purgatory springs!" No wonder Martin Luther blew his top and nailed on a church door his vigorous challenges to priestly usurpation of God's grace. Roman Catholics subsequently backed off from an embarrassing commercialization of what originated as a compassionate concern for people. The punitive aspect of purgatory faded into the background, although prayers for the dead continue, as a way to bond the church terrestrial with the church celestial.[18]

Final sanctification at death. In reaction to these abuses within the medieval church, "protestant" Christians rejected this doctrine of punitive purgatory and generally concluded that in the "article of death" believers are instantaneously purified from whatever remains of sinful propensity or habit. They exalted a theology of grace against what they considered an unbiblical doctrine of works-righteousness. The righteousness of Christ suffices. This continues to be a tenet of Reformed churches.

John Calvin envisioned immediate transition into heaven—no punishment or purgation. God's sovereign power cleanses the elect. Calvin urged Christians to overcome a natural fear of dying. "If we reflect that this our tabernacle, unstable, defective, corruptible, fading, pining, and putrid, is dissolved," he wrote, "in order that it may forthwith be renewed in sure, perfect, incorruptible, in fine, in heavenly glory, will not faith compel us eagerly to desire what nature dreads?"[19]

Sanctification complete in this life. To some critics Reformed theology seemed to stultify moral effort, induce spiritual sloth, and presume upon God's grace, leaving persons comfortably sinful. Robert Barclay, a seventeenth-century theologian, challenged the Westminster Confession, which asserted that no one can keep God's commandments perfectly, that even the best actions, thoughts, and prayers of the saints are impure and polluted. Barclay criticized this view as neglecting imparted righteousness. He asserted, to the contrary, that the Holy Spirit cleanses believers from the "body of death" and gives power to overcome sin, citing 1 John 3:9 (NIV): "No one who is born of God will continue to sin." Barclay affirmed a level of perfection sufficient to keep one from transgressing the law of God and permitting one to do what God requires.[20]

John Wesley, a century later, believed the Calvinist view to be inadequate. Although he agreed that most persons who have died in faith have not been "perfected in love," he believed that more *could* be, that if in the "article of death" entire sanctification must occur, why not sooner for those who seek it? He supported his views by biblical references such as Jesus' high-priestly prayer recorded in John 17, and other exhortations to "be perfect," arguing that we wouldn't be commanded to do something impossible to attain.[21] One can say that Wesley started from the premise that perfection must occur no later than the moment of death and worked backward in time, whereas Barclay started from the premise that perfection is inherent within the new birth and worked forward, both emphasizing the provisions of God's sanctifying grace to impart righteousness and prepare one for eternal life.

Reformed and holiness theologies define sin differently, the former including in that definition any transgression of God's law, the latter "voluntary transgression of the known will of God." If the Calvinist view can induce moral complacency by persons presuming upon divine grace, the holiness view can induce spiritual pride by persons rationalizing to their favor what is God's will. Both views, however, affirm growth in sanctification in this life. Both affirm the believer's bliss upon entering heaven, without need for punitive correction.

Hell as purgation. As noted above, hell is considered an interim state by some Christians—those who believe that God's love will ultimately overpower the most recalcitrant sinners. Hindu Vedic literature likewise views hell as temporary, believing it to be an interim state through which souls driven by the vices of desire, anger, and greed must pass during the cycle of rebirth. Sinners may be subject to torments (such as being crushed, burned, boiled, or pecked by vultures) during these states.[22] Islamic tradition envisions a bridge spanning Gehenna, the top layer of hell (the Fire), upon which the saved and the condemned must travel after the judgment. Although the saved move across easily and the condemned quickly fall, some with faith to their credit fall into the Fire for limited times of purgation.[23]

Purgatory as preparation. If theologians too neatly separate sanctification from justification, will people presume upon God's grace? Historically, the answer has been yes: people are tempted to presume upon grace as a cover for sin. William Penn lamented that people were sinning more freely "at Christ's cost," and in our era Dietrich Bonhoeffer deplored "cheap grace." Fearing such antinomianism, some Christians have held to a more inclusive understanding of God's power, both to forgive sins and to purge the disposition to sin. Jerry L. Walls believes that a case can be made for purgatory for everyone, not as punishment but as a time for completing the process of sanctification. Walls considers that a theology of holiness makes this more logical than positing temporary punishment, as in the Roman Catholic tradition, or affirming instantaneous completion of sanctification "at the article of death," as in Reformed theology. He finds his views to resemble those of Orthodoxy and considers himself an ally of C. S. Lewis.[24]

I affirm Walls's position in general but question whether the term *purgatory* can be adapted to convey such expected discipline. If Christian discipleship means being under the tutelage of Christ, and we continue to be disciples in heaven, then some sort of training for entrants may be in order (a sort of "in-service schooling"). This would seem to be the case especially because many persons reach the afterlife in a state of immaturity. Furthermore, considering the numbers of people and their diversity, humanity has a lot of misconceptions and biases to get rid of, many insights to gain. Humility is a virtue for all of us, at all levels of finitude, so training in discipleship will occur in heaven, not in some anteroom or holding pen. We will accept such discipline readily, joyously, in the holy fear of the Lord, not considering it to be punishment or ourselves to be second-class citizens, because ego lovingly submits to Deo. As the Psalmist said, "The fear of the Lord is the beginning of wisdom" (Ps. 111:10).

FOUR

Evidences for Heaven

Just as I believe the Book of Scripture illumines the
pathway to God, so I believe that the Book of Nature,
with its astonishing details . . . also suggests a God of
purpose and a God of design. And I think my belief
makes me no less a scientist.[1]
—*Owen Gingerich*

Heaven is in a world beyond, just on the other side of a
thin veil of time. If you could close your eyes and walk
through that veil, you could be there. It is that close.[2]
—*Joseph F. Girzone*

In the second chapter I posited that heaven is most coherently
understood as a reality congruent with creation, and in the
third I explored how God prepares us for eternal life. Now we
consider prospects for reaching and exploring our eternal home,
the city of God, the heavenly Jerusalem.

When anticipating moving into territory of uncertain location,
we typically first make sure the place exists and then we determine

how to get there. We study maps to trace routes and destination sites. On the way we look out for reliable road signs. If we discover paths or roads, we infer a destination. At crossroads we take care to remain on the right course. Along the way occasionally we pull over to the side of the road to rest and to review information we've gleaned ahead of time about who and what we hope to find there. We envision ourselves in our new homeland. If someone we trust has been to this destination, and recommends it, we have confidence that our journey will not be in vain, that it will fulfill our highest expectations.

We're *all* on life's journey to an uncertain location. Wherever and however we move about now on this earth, this much is certain: that journey will take us *through the valley of the shadow of death*. What lies beyond?

Here's what a trusted friend, Jesus, told his followers: "There are many rooms in my Father's house; if it were not so, I would have told you. I am going there to prepare a place for you. And if I go and prepare a place for you, I will come back and take you to be with me that you also may be where I am" (John 14:2–3, NIV). In the light of all Jesus said and did, his atoning death, and especially his resurrection, it doesn't seem credible that Jesus was speaking euphemistically about followers joining him in a sacrificial death honored by posterity. No, Jesus' words signify a gathering at a real location. I trust his word. Angela of Foligno, friend of Francis of Assisi, in a vision heard the voice of Jesus say, "My love for you has not been a hoax."[3] This friend speaks my mind!

What evidences are there for heaven as an actual place for personal life after death? They're diverse, but they demonstrate a pattern of coherence that sustains our hope. Picture that pattern of proof as an arch. An arch is an effective engineering design, whether used in Gothic cathedrals or in present-day highway bridges. In its simplicity of design an arch is both beautiful and useful. Now picture the resurrection of Christ as the keystone in that arch, and other evidences as lower or higher tiers of stone resting on a foundation of *purposeful intelligence*. Rising from the base on one side at a lower level, the evidence consists of *persistent and diverse cultural intuitions,* and at a higher level *scriptural revelations affirming an afterlife.* Rising from the base on the other side at a lower level, the evidence consists of *personal otherworldly experiences,* and at a higher level *the testimony of the witnesses to Jesus' resurrection.* Finally, picture *corroborative personal spiritual experience* as the superstructure dependent upon and affirming the integrity of the arch. Such a superstructure constitutes a "cathedral of the spirit," or a bridge across the abyss of death and despair.

With this architectural metaphor in mind, let's examine the "stones" that sustain our hopes of heaven. We begin by considering the foundation, then the "stones" rising from it. Then, changing the order a bit, we'll examine the key evidence—Jesus' resurrection—followed by the testimony of those who witnessed it. Finally, we'll examine the superstructure of corroborative personal spiritual experience.

PURPOSEFUL INTELLIGENCE

The presence of intelligence in nature implies an underlying purpose in the universe. Whether purposeful intelligence implies *divine origin,* however, has been argued for centuries (in teleological and cosmological arguments too extensive to include in this book).[4] In any case, the universal nature of intelligence offers a basis for positing its eternal quality; it indicates that everlasting life is at least a reasonable and viable implication.

We can't deny that intelligence is present and pervasive. We find it in animals to varying degrees and eminently in human beings. Some persons think plants exhibit a modicum of intelligence and may even respond to sensitive "green thumb" folks. In recent decades scientists have been probing the universe for signals that intelligence exists elsewhere in the cosmos. SETI (Search for Extraterrestrial Intelligence) is an organization dedicated to this pursuit.[5] So far, no convincing evidence has been recorded by the various electronic probes; but who knows when it might occur? At least we know *one* world that (on balance) gives evidence for intelligent purpose—earth. If there weren't intelligence, we wouldn't be able to label certain actions as stupid or irrational. Or to look for life on other planets. Or to philosophize about how we know, what we know, and the worth of what we know.[6] Or to ponder the issues of this book.

Anthropologist Teilhard de Chardin fittingly entitled a book about the explosive spread of intelligence *The Phenomenon of Man*. By whatever process intelligence arrived, whether by fiat or evolutionary process, by slow accretions or catastrophic events, it's present now as an incontrovertible reality. Many respected scientists affirm the "anthropic principle"—namely, that the whole cosmos seems specifically designed for humanity. One of those scientists, John Polkinghorne, defines the principle in this way: "A universe capable of evolving carbon-based life is a very particular universe indeed, 'finely tuned' in the character of its basic physical processes. . . . [T]his insight is called the 'Anthropic Principle.' Not any old world is capable of producing *anthropi*, beings of a complexity comparable to that of humankind. . . . Our universe represents a very tiny fertile patch in what is otherwise a desert area of possibilities."[7]

The first quotation at the head of this chapter is from Harvard astronomer Owen Gingerich, who finds supernatural design credible to his science and congenial to his faith in God. A British colleague, Nobel Prize–winner Sir John Eccles, has written definitive studies of the brain. He describes levels of purpose in the genetic structure of organisms and believes that self-consciousness, in particular, reflects divine creation. He concludes: "In some mysterious way, God is the Creator of all the living forms in the evolutionary process, and particularly in hominid evolution of human persons, each with the conscious selfhood of an immortal soul. On this transcendent vision we have to build our lives with self-conscious purpose."[8]

Significantly, in the prologue to his Gospel, New Testament writer John used the term *Logos,* "Word," for Christ, conveying the purposefulness and coherence of both creation and redemption. "In the beginning was the Word. . . ." Purposeful intelligence is foundational for the hope of heaven.

PERSISTENT CULTURAL INTUITIONS

The pervasiveness in culture of belief in an afterlife doesn't conclusively prove its reality, but it heightens credibility. It makes heaven a reasonable hope. It's more than a good bet. This is so because variant, noncollusive testimonies in support of a shared conviction increase the probability of that conviction's truth. "Homesickness for heaven" pervades stories and rituals of all human cultures, often with no indication of cross-cultural exchanges.

For example, the ancient Chinese rulers used terracotta statues of their retainers and their animals to enshrine their hopes of an afterlife not unlike earthly existence. Uncovered in recent years at Xian, these statues are now a major tourist attraction. The Aztecs developed elaborate rituals for the dead, providing bowls of water to sustain the deceased on the journey, and ritually burning prize baskets. Aztec poets lamented the loss of flowers in the land where the "fleshless" ones dwell. The Toltecs, who honored the sage Quetzalcoatl as a god, believed that certain hairless dogs carried the meritorious dead across to the next world; and when a ruler died, male and female slaves were slain so that they could continue making chocolate for their master in the next world.[9] (Oh, the power of chocolate!)

For all their cruelty, such rituals illustrate a terrible and persistent hunger for eternal life in ancient cultures. Note the poignant yearning expressed in this ancient Mexican poem:

> *Beyond is the place where one lives.*
> *I would be lying to myself were I to say,*
> *"Perhaps everything ends on this earth;*
> *here do our lives end."*
> *No, O Lord of the Close Vicinity,*
> *it is beyond, with those who dwell in Your house,*
> *that I will sing songs to You, in the innermost heaven.*
> *My heart rises;*
> *I fix my eyes upon You,*
> *next to you, beside You,*
> *O Giver of Life!* [10]

Freudians consider such intuitions of immortality nothing but misplaced illusions. Their views are no longer widely shared, however. Indeed, those views strike many of us now as elitist and parochial. Yearnings for eternal life, however crudely or cruelly expressed, cannot be reduced to sexual fantasies. Intuitions differ around the world, from myths of eternal return to popular stories about the afterlife, but they abound. Stories about a special race of diminutive people—leprechauns, elves, and the like—also cross cultures; they're found in Inuit as well as Celtic societies, for example. If persistent transcultural accounts of "little people" imply prehistorical phenomena not presently documented (as many people allege), how much more might persistent transcultural accounts of heaven point toward a reality difficult to comprehend empirically but less difficult to know intuitively?

Popular notions about heaven shouldn't be dismissed as "just metaphors." As a poet I bristle at such denigration. Metaphors often illuminate reality through poetic analogy more clearly than does prosaic language through inductive/deductive logic. Have you noticed how scientific hypotheses use metaphor to interpret data? For example, scientists picture light as both "wave" and "particle." Consider an ordinary example of analogy using the metaphoric language of a simile. The poetic line "My love is like a red, red rose" applies qualities of beauty to an actual person. It makes the point more aptly than saying, "My love is five-foot-two, weighs 130 pounds, and has body parts that are not only intact but quite symmetrical."

Love is a quality; a loved one is a living entity. Heaven is not a quality; it's a metaphysical entity. Metaphor signifies more than a synonym for a character quality. Analogies such as "the bosom of Abraham," or "paradise," or "the throne of God" signify a reality difficult to define because it transcends ordinary experience. Hence signs convey the nature of its reality by qualities couched in metaphor, such as *caring, comfort,* and *power.* They signify that heaven is a metaphysical ground for such values, not a synonym for them. One can't say that heaven is 140 miles southwest of Portland, Oregon (although one can say that Yachats is, and that it's a "heavenly" coastal town!). But one *can* say that heaven is like a scenic earthly place, only more so.

An awareness of afterlife is an aspect of human self-consciousness. Acknowledging culture as a repository and conveyer of truth adds evidence to claims for heaven's reality. The foundation of purposeful intelligence may be covered with mud and the supporting stones with briars by these cultural intuitions about heaven, but they can be discovered!

Otherworldly experiences include psychic claims and near-death experiences. Psychic claims for contacts between persons living and persons dead stand as untested but persistent testimony to the reality of heaven. At best these claims strengthen plausibility; at worst they foster skepticism by confusing fantasy with genuine intuition. When I proposed writing this book my wife asked, half-jokingly, "Why not just get in touch with Jack Willcuts? [He's a longtime friend who died a dozen years ago.] Ask *him* what heaven's like."

Well, I'm generally skeptical of séances, wary of hype, and vigilant against hypnotic exploitation of human emotions. The one biblical story about a medium reinforces my wariness. It seems that a floundering king, Saul, used a medium, a woman of Endor, to contact the deceased prophet Samuel. From reading the account in 1 Samuel 28, I surmise that the whole thing ended badly. Conniving to get the dead to bail out the living apparently isn't something God looks on favorably. So I don't think those of us on this side of the chasm ought to be trying to ring up those on the other side. How about them contacting us? Well, that may be different.

A few times over a long life I've experienced the presence of a deceased person. You may have, too. Years ago, after the accidental drowning of a friend, David Thomas, it seemed that one day he stood by me and said, "It's okay, Arthur." I was startled, but then comforted and reassured. It wasn't something that could be laboratory-tested as a repeatable occurrence; but it was an intimation of immortality, a flicker of light in the shadow of death. The poignant love story of Sheldon and Jean Vanauken, *A Severe Mercy*, includes an account in which, two years after her untimely death, Jean ("Davy") comes to her bereaved husband from heaven in a vision. They hold each other "cheek to cheek" and she reassures him of her continued presence with him. It was a situation, Vanauken writes, "pervaded with bliss."[11]

Testimonies about near-death experiences, as Moody, Kübler-Ross, Wills-Brandon, and others have narrated and interpreted, deserve respectful attention. Clinical tests have been conducted that tend to affirm the phenomena, whatever the interpretation. Gary R. Habermas and J. P. Moreland discuss these phenomena and offer a faith perspective in a recent publication, *Beyond Death*.[12] People hovering at the border between life and death report tunnels leading to wondrous light, and other blissful experiences. For example, Dr. Wills-Brandon relates a story of a dying eleven-year-old boy, who suddenly saw Jesus in the room and exclaimed about how beautiful things were and about being able finally to do a double jump-rope.[13]

It's as hard to explain away testimonies of near-death experiences as it is to explain them. Some people assert scientific explanations for these events, such as trauma-imaging arising from chemical reactions in the brain. Others in the scientific community, however, have concluded that the mind can't be reduced to brain waves.[14] People who have hovered between life and death are likewise unconvinced by reductive explanations.

In response to the difficulty of assessing such phenomena empirically, some atheists have posited explanations about lingering selfhood. Others, less inclined toward treating "auras" as scientific, have moved from atheism to a troubled agnosticism. Such troubled agnostic openness is commendable. After all, honest doubt is the underside of thoughtful faith. The father of a child Jesus healed cried out, "I believe; help my unbelief" (Mark 9:24). In similar fashion we pray when confronted with what looks to be miraculous. To summarize, beatific visions of an afterlife offer convergent testimony that heaven is a credible hope.

SCRIPTURAL REVELATION

Scriptural revelation rests upon the foundation of purposeful intelligence. It bears the marks of divine truth more definitively and prescriptively than the truths found in cultural intuitions. See Appendix A for a listing of scriptural verses affirming eternal life.

With other theists I believe that the Scriptures are God's word written. They provide an authoritative context for truths gleaned through God's word revealed in nature and in history. They authenticate God's voice in our hearts and minds. By them we test creeds and other religious pronouncements. The "word of Scripture" provides teachings central for belief in heaven and intimations concerning its nature. These basic teachings include the following:

- The creation is good, not evil; sin springs from the will, not the body.
- Humanity is made in God's image; we're all stewards of creation.
- Sin has marred that image and damaged creation.
- God is redeeming humanity and renewing creation.
- God's kingdom has come, but is more fully coming.
- Jesus fulfills other covenants of God with humanity.
- Jesus' death and resurrection are central to human redemption.
- The biblical witness and interpretations offer a true and faithful record.
- The church is called to testify to these acts of God.

THE RESURRECTION OF JESUS

The resurrection of Jesus is central to Christian beliefs about the afterlife. Exactly what occurred in Jesus' resurrection is difficult fully to comprehend, although some things in the New Testament account are clear and compelling. Jesus was crucified on a Roman cross. He died. On the third day after his death the tomb into which he had been sealed was empty. Thereafter the risen Jesus appeared to followers on several occasions, coming and going mysteriously for several weeks: he ate food with them; he blessed them and bestowed upon them his Spirit; he charged them to spread the good news of God's redemption from sin; he urged them to live as his followers in God's kingdom, promising to reappear on earth to lead that kingdom. Then, disappearing from their sensory milieu, he "ascended into heaven." (Appendix A, referred to previously as listing references to eternal life, also contains a listing of relevant New Testament passages about the resurrection.)

Early skeptics (suppressing evidence from frightened soldiers) claimed that the resurrection story was a hoax—that the disciples had hidden the body; present-day skeptics claim that the early church made up the resurrection account, along with miraculous birth stories, to rationalize the failure of their hero, Jesus. There's no evidence at all for such spin-doctoring.[15] Instead, these conjectures reflect a bias of unbelief and a self-serving effort by leaders to accommodate Christianity to a culture of unbelief.

Why have some scholars within the community of faith downplayed or even discredited what has been historically the central doctrine of the Christian faith? Carol Zaleski thinks she knows why. In her Ingersoll Lecture at Harvard University in 2000, Professor Zaleski stated that although approximately eighty percent of Americans believe in life after death, the percentage is much lower for academically trained religious thinkers. This disparity troubles her, she said, for it puts the burden of proof upon the believer, not the skeptic, and lays upon ordinary worshipers an onus of selfish motive. Many academic scholars, she noted, have simply ruled out immortality as something no reasonable person believes anymore. If asked why, they muster up objections to immortality "on moral grounds as self-aggrandizing, on psychological grounds as self-deceiving, and on philosophical grounds as dualistic. Concern for the soul is faulted for making us disregard the body, neglect our responsibilities for the earth, and deny our kinship with other life forms."

Zaleski answers these objections succinctly and makes a reasoned case for recovering beliefs in immortality, which she categorizes as follows:

On an ascending scale of historical or cultural beliefs she considers the highest level to be "Omega immortality" biblical and rational, affirming the central insight of Jewish and Christian eschatologies. Its premises: "[H]uman beings are creatures, composite of dust and God's animating breath," and they're immortal because they bear the stamp of God's image. Immortality "is a sheer gift." About continuing personal identity she asks and answers this rhetorical question: "How will I know it is the same me? . . . [B]ecause I will see the same Him." Zaleski believes that this view of immortality answers cultural aspirations, and in Christ offers both personal and social aspects of salvation. "Our ancestors were afraid of hell," she laments; "we are afraid of heaven." She urges adoration, submission, and love for God as ways to make heaven look exciting.[16]

In the Ingersoll Lecture for 2001–2002, Huston Smith, an eminent authority on world religions, offered a sequel to Zaleski's provocative earlier lecture. From a more sociological perspective he noted three case studies "that might soften the current prejudices against immortality." These three are: Swedenborg's visions of heaven, near-death experiences, and entheogen (drug-induced visions of a nonmaterial world). Smith's case studies suggest "there are empirical as well as theoretical reasons for thinking that the wager is not an irrational bet."[17] I've already noted that near-death experiences have some evidential value. I'm less inclined than Smith to include drug-induced visions, however, although as empirical events hallucinations may offer fractured pictures of reality. I'd be more inclined to accept the phenomena of religious visions as offering glimpses into eternity. The esoteric visions of Swedenborg, an eccentric eighteenth-century Swedish theologian, fueled the speculations of several nineteenth-century American cultic movements, most of which neglected his biblical orientation. Cultural intuitions and scriptural insights often get mixed in strange combinations! In any case, in his visions Swedenborg did foresee heaven as a place for real things and embodied persons.

The disjuncture between science and theology that developed in the Enlightenment of the eighteenth century had the effect of restricting faith-claims to qualitative states of mind, as noted earlier, putting religious studies in parallel with psychology, sociology, and anthropology in assessing the human condition. In this academic milieu religion in general, and specific doctrines such as the resurrection of Jesus in particular, became viewed as mythic activity, providing rituals of social accommodation, not necessarily related to empirical data. In a commendable but misguided effort to be "objective" in respect to religious history, scholars often swept away all traces of the miraculous.

In recent years there has been a new round of scholarship re-examining the historical Jesus. Some of these Jesus studies seem to indicate an academic yen for revisionist history; others smack of pandering to media-driven quests for novelty. In a secular marketplace the periphery of religious tradition is more newsworthy than its center. (The first Christian apologists faced this inordinate yen for novelty in Athens.) Despite these negative aspects, some positive values have emerged from the recent quest for the historical Jesus. For example, the quest offers insights neglected by a church that focuses too restrictively upon Christ as Savior only, and not also upon Christ as Lord. My colleague Paul Anderson, a leading Johannine scholar, notes that through these studies "the historical Jesus, as well as the risen Christ, is understood rightly to be a challenger of the status quo even when it bears the name Christian." Anderson believes that "the present leadership of the risen Christ" is bolstered by some of the recent portraits of Jesus, and prophetically chides scholars thus: "Let the seeker of the historical Jesus beware! The truest form of knowing may indeed imply coming to know experientially."[18]

Some of the ancient arguments against Jesus' resurrection have resurfaced in recent times (as they have periodically over the centuries)—for example, his disciples spirited him away, or another person was hanged in his stead as God snatched his prophet away. More relevant to our discussion is the view, held by some sincere Christian scholars today, that Jesus died a heroic, even atoning death, but that his appearances to the disciples were visionary only (though those visions were so compelling and God-directed that the church was born as a result, as witness to God's power to redeem humanity). After all, if spiritual reality is more important than physical reality, does it really matter whether Jesus' body disintegrated in a different grave? Does it matter if his bones might be unearthed by some future archeologist?[19] To affirm a purely spiritual resurrection seems to some scholars a way to salvage central Christian beliefs within a scientific milieu that otherwise might render Christianity obsolete. To them it's intellectually appropriate to eschew dogma and focus upon spiritual renewal in doing the work of God's kingdom, instead of laboring to rest the case for Christianity on shaky ground.

Most Christian scholars, however, consider the physical resurrection of Jesus to be a God-chosen mode of revelation, an event central to history and central to kingdom spirituality.[20] Additionally, in respect to the theme of this book, the resurrection of Jesus testifies to heaven as a realm of reality and not just a guiding principle for the good life.

Recently there occurred a debate, first at Boston College and then in print, between two scholars who differ sharply about the resurrection of Jesus. William Lane Craig, a Christian philosopher and professor at Talbot School of Theology, affirms the resurrection against Gerd Lüdemann, an atheist New Testament scholar at the University of Göttingen, who disavows it. Other scholars in the debate support or modify arguments. In his concluding remarks Lüdemann acknowledges the need for spirituality but now finds it as a humanist rather than as a Christian. Drawing from the Nag Hammadi texts, he posits resurrection as only a symbol for what remains stable and enduring. He claims that the Christian myth "has been refuted historically once and for all"[21] and is comfortable with a non-theistic affirmation of universal values.

Craig, on the other hand, in his closing statement, rejects the notion that moral values can be sustained by a naturalistic worldview. He calls it the "Noble Lie"—elitist, self-serving, and without rational foundation. He rejects efforts by liberal theologians to salvage value from the resurrection while rejecting it as an event. "If God exists," he writes, "then value and meaning have a sure, transcendent foundation in God himself. More than that, it becomes a live option to believe that this transcendent Creator has acted immanently in the world to reveal his love and purpose to us. Jesus of Nazareth claimed to be just such a revelation of God. If God raised him from the dead, then we have good reason to listen to his claims."[22]

One of the scholars supporting the resurrection as historical and actual is Stephen T. Davis, a philosopher at Claremont McKenna College. In his conclusion he expresses admiration for Lüdemann's honesty but challenges his data and interpretations. "There are contemporary scholars in theology and in New

Testament," Davis notes, "who cannot bring themselves to accept the claim that God raised Jesus from the dead." In contrast with Lüdemann's candor, they "hide behind arcane theological language, designed (or so it seems) more to obfuscate than to communicate."[23]

Most Christian scholars over the centuries and currently have repudiated the assertions of such obfuscating skeptics. The *nature* of the resurrected life has been open to various interpretations, but not generally the credibility of the event itself. A century after Paul, a Christian convert, the lawyer Tertullian wrote this: "For to Christ was it reserved to lay bare everything which before was concealed: to impart certainty to doubtful points; to accomplish those of which men had had but a foretaste; to give present reality to the objects of prophecy; and to furnish not only by Himself, but actually in Himself, certain proofs of the resurrection of the dead."[24] A second-century Athenian philosopher, Athenagoras, defended Christians against persecution on trumped-up and slanderous charges of atheism, incest, and cannibalism. He contrasted a disregard for life arising from hedonic philosophy ("Eat, drink, and be merry, for tomorrow we die") with a high regard for life arising from Christian faith (as in, for example, the injunction to return good for evil). The Christians, he said, "know that the life for which we look is better than can be told, if we arrive at it pure from all wrongdoing."[25]

A second-century scholar from Samaria, Justin, at the cost of his life, gave this witness: "The resurrection is a resurrection of the flesh which died. For the spirit dies not; the soul is in the body, and without a soul it cannot live. The body, when the soul forsakes it, is not. For the body is the house of the soul, and the soul the house of the spirit. These three, in all who cherish a sincere hope and unquestioning faith in God, will be saved."[26] Justin's holistic view of human nature sounds quite contemporary!

Confidence in eternal life in heaven has marked the testimony of the church through all the centuries, and this testimony has engendered a high regard for life on earth as well as in heaven. Despite its backsliding into holy wars and inquisitions, despite its sadly misplaced zeal, Christianity has provided a foundation for high morality, deeds of compassion, and just governance. The good news of eternal life produced the church and laid the foundation for righteousness, in this life and the next.

We live in a new age of empire. As in the Greco-Roman era, cultural creativity and intellectual brilliance contrast starkly with cultural depravity and ignorance. Violence marks our world, as it did the one in which the early Christians lived. Poverty lies in chilly shadows cast by towering wealth and technological structures. Paganism abounds, too, unsophisticated and sophisticated. But the words of Christian thinkers are being heard again in the marketplace, in academia, among those who govern, and by those who buy and sell, as were the words of Tertullian, Justin, and Athenagoras. Empires rise and fall, as Luther said, but God's Word—Jesus—abides. Consider the words of a pair of contemporary Christian apologists. Along with others cited elsewhere in this book, they affirm Jesus' resurrection.

Jürgen Moltmann, a respected German biblical scholar, affirms a physical resurrection. He believes that God created the world not out of inner necessity, but out of love. "The human being lives *wholly*," he writes, "the *whole* human being dies, God will *wholly* raise the human being."[27] An equally respected British scientist, John Polkinghorne, concurs. He writes:

> The resurrection of Christ is not something that can be established beyond a peradventure, or understood in a completely straightforward way. If it happened, it is the most significant event in all history and it carries with it profound implications

for who Jesus really was. If it did not happen, Christianity is either deluded or reduced to a kind of pious wishing that it had been so. It is not easy to say precisely what "happen" means for so unique an event, but its significance turns on the truth or falsehood of the fundamental Christian claim that "Jesus lives!" No one can convince the skeptical against their will, but there is both significant historical and theological motivation for the belief. It is a belief held by the writer of this book.[28]

Scientists search for a "unified field theory" to explain everything. God's word—in nature, in Scripture, and in the human heart—may be that unifying theory. And Jesus' resurrection validates that divine word.

An oft-quoted remark by astronomer Robert Jastrow in a 1978 lecture may need to be revised. He wrote, "For the scientist who has lived by his faith in the power of reason, the story [of the exploration of the beginning of the universe] ends like a bad dream. He has scaled the mountains of ignorance; he is about to conquer the highest peak; as he pulls himself over the final rock, he is greeted by a band of theologians who have been sitting there for centuries."[29] A sequel to this story might now read, "As the theologian who lived by his ability to adapt divine mysteries to scientific rationality scales the highest academic ladder in the quest for universal truth, he is greeted by a coterie of cosmologists and biologists joyously praising the redemptive mysteries of God, the Creator."

TESTIMONY OF THE WITNESSES

We turn now to those whose testimony is preserved in Scripture. The biblical account shows that the first witnesses were scared out of their wits by the empty tomb, and by the angel(s) who sat by the tomb and told startled followers: "He is not here; he has risen"

(Luke 24:6, NIV). Jesus' resurrection was harder for Jesus' followers to understand than his tragic and cruel death. Death they could handle with anointing spices and tears of grief. But life beyond the grave? This was hard to comprehend, even after the miracles Jesus had performed, even after his teaching about the kingdom of God and his reassurances that he was going to prepare a place in heaven for them. And yet no cooked-up testimony came from these witnesses—rather, convincing reports, varying in detail but agreeing in substance. No collusion, no manufactured stories, because the Gospel testimony came from people who were *there*.

Jesus' appearances among the believers exhibited a tension between the tangible and the intangible. Jesus touched certain of his followers, broke bread with them, spoke to them. Their senses were alive to his presence, as they were before the crucifixion. And yet Jesus had changed; he was different. He appeared in various forms, coming and going out of the range of their dimensionality. Their senses, reason, and intuition became intermingled in heightened acuity. No wonder they were astonished, confused, and even afraid.

Michael Welker, a theologian from the University of Heidelberg, comments on this tension and articulates what the witnesses experienced:

> The reality of the resurrection is more than a simply natural event. This reality concerns the human species more deeply, it is more powerful than merely natural events. Here we encounter the resurrected Christ who has overcome death. Here we have before us not simply an earthly person who can only be present in one place and time. Here we meet with the resurrected and elevated Christ who can and does reveal himself in diverse forms and in surprising ways at many places. This reality of the resurrection is no illusion, no product of the fantasy. It is borne wit-

ness to by many men and women, and in many different contexts of experience. All the witnesses refer back to the historical Jesus and the fullness of his life. They all refer to his past and to his future.[30]

Welker rightly insists that it's not the *memory* of those events that makes the resurrection account in the New Testament compelling, but rather the "substance and the glory of the life of Christ incarnate."[31] These witnesses to the resurrection experienced Christ inwardly, and so have Christians throughout the centuries following.

One person not present at any of the various resurrection appearances, but who experienced the risen Christ dramatically a few years later, was a prominent Pharisee, Saul, who became Paul the evangelist. What Paul wrote to the church in Corinth is what Christians have experienced of Christ's redemptive power throughout the ages, and have witnessed by deed and word:

Now if Christ is proclaimed as raised from the dead, how can some of you say there is no resurrection of the dead? If there is no resurrection of the dead, then Christ has not been raised; and if Christ has not been raised, then our proclamation has been in vain and your faith has been in vain. We are even found to be misrepresenting God, because we testified of God that he raised Christ—whom he did not raise if it is true that the dead are not raised. For if the dead are not raised, then Christ has not been raised. If Christ has not been raised, your faith is futile and you are still in your sins. Then those also who have died in Christ have perished. If for this life only we have hoped in Christ, we are of all people most to be pitied. But in fact Christ has been raised from the dead, the first fruits of those who have died. (1 Cor. 15:12–20)

CORROBORATIVE PERSONAL EXPERIENCE

For thousands of years believers have experienced God in such emotionally compelling ways that they can readily accept resurrection as consistent with those experiences. They consider that their hopes are not only credible but also experiential. Hope of heaven gives life coherent meaning, as the above quotation from Paul underscored. From the questing of Job to the doubting of Thomas, hope in resurrection is a trusted bridge across troubled terrain and through thick darkness. Death seems to persons of faith, in the words of the poet John Greenleaf Whittier, "but a covered way which opens into light."[32]

In communities of faith in diverse cultures and circumstances throughout human history, thousands of persons, many quite recently, have gone to their death as martyrs testifying to this hope. Their highest allegiance, these believers have insisted, is to the kingdom of God, not to empires or nations, tribes or races, corporations or neighborhoods of this world. Their experiences of and insights about the kingdom of God—present but yet to come—have provided the motivation and vision that help earthly realms approximate the heavenly model. This vision of a human life redeemed now and gifted with eternity has changed the course of history. The yeast of heaven has stimulated deeds of heroism and dedicated compassion. The spotlight of heaven has called evil into judgment and brought righteousness to the public square. On April 2, 1945, from the Dachau prison camp, Martin Niemöller shared Easter thoughts with his fellow prisoners. The resurrection of Jesus "can only be certified through testimony," he said. The Berlin pastor had confidence that through the risen Christ "a way is opened before us, a way out from this terrestrial world of sin and death, a way into the eternal divine world of peace and life."[33]

Quite regularly Christian worshipers pray aloud together as Jesus taught the first disciples: "Thy will be done on earth as it is in heaven." Surely this means that heaven exists in a more definitive reality than what we now know on earth! Otherwise, how could it be a model, and not just projected idealism? Belief in the afterlife is reaffirmed at funerals and memorials and at Easter-time throughout the world. Believers have testified to it with words and deeds—sometimes clumsily, sometimes effectively, often heroically.

I mentioned earlier that we look forward to visiting a place a trusted friend commends to us. For Christians that trusted friend is Jesus and the place to be explored after death is heaven. For us Jesus is more than a name in history, more than a heroic prophet, more than a renowned teacher. Jesus is a *present*, not a distant, Savior. We don't just *know about* Jesus; we *know him*. Joyfully we proclaim, "What a friend we have in Jesus!" We've found Jesus to be right about things pertaining to life on earth, and we're confident that he's right about life in heaven, too. General evidences for eternal life offer plausibility. Our friend Jesus Christ offers promise. Christ's presence in the heart and in the community of faith confirms that promise. That presence quickens expectations and removes fears. Christ within and among us is, indeed, our hope of glory! In worship, fellowship, and service we now experience aspects of God's eternal kingdom—righteousness, peace, joy—and we long for more. Supremely, we anticipate exploring heaven because Christ beckons us there! He summons humanity into the renewed world God is preparing. A prophet greater than Moses, Jesus the Messiah leads humanity across its multiple and sundry deserts and over barrier rivers into the cosmic and eternal Promised Land.

In my youth I sang a hymn of commitment to this friend and to God's vision for a redeemed humanity in a restored universe: "Where He leads me I will follow—I'll go with Him, with Him, all the way." I'm singing it now in my mind and heart. Join me, if you wish.

FIVE

The Inhabitants of Heaven

There will come a time when every culture, every institution, every nation, the human race, all biological life, is extinct, and every one of us is still alive. Immortality is promised to us, not to these generalities. . . . [W]e are assured of our eternal self-identity and shall live to remember the galaxies as an old tale.[1]

—*C. S. Lewis*

In the resurrected Me, my deepest being comes rushing free at last and with it "all my winters turn to spring."[2]

—*Pearl Crist Hall*

I agree with C. S. Lewis in the first epigraph, above, if he's stressing the wonder and magnitude of personal eternal life, but I must disagree if he means that God plans to replace things with thought. As the Bible clearly affirms, the created, material world is good, though now marred by sin. It will be renewed in righteousness. So I affirm Pearl Hall's metaphor of renewal.

In the second chapter I made the case that heaven is a reality congruent with the created world. That chapter answered questions that arise from our need to understand heaven in categories of space. The third chapter explicated eternal life, answering questions that arise from our need to understand heaven in categories of time. The fourth chapter examined the evidences and concluded that heaven can be acknowledged credibly as an integral and central part of divine creation. Resurrected bodies are congruent with enhanced (not diminished) materiality. Limiting immortality to souls lacks integrity with divine creation. This present chapter concerns the terrain of heaven and its inhabitants. Subsequent chapters will suggest how persons participate in an environment in which they can plan and do things, can be engaged with one another in the Blessed Community to which the church is witness, and serve God in the creation of a renewed cosmos.

THE TERRAIN OF HEAVEN

Our earth revolves around one sun spinning on the edge of the Milky Way, one planet swirling among billions of other stars in this particular galaxy. Where in that vast expanse of space is heaven? Is it within this galaxy or another, or is it beyond the known celestial realm? Would it not be more logical to consider heaven as an order of reality in which creatures interact freely and creatively with their sovereign Creator *throughout* the present cosmos or succeeding ones—forever?

In Chapter Nine we will inquire more closely about the shape of such cosmic renewal. For now it's enough to say that exploring the terrain of heaven doesn't mean we wave goodbye to planet Terra at the end of the age. The Bible forecasts a renovation of our part of the cosmos after a time of final judgment and catastrophe.

Christians hold that the second coming of Christ will usher in the kingdom of God on earth. Biblical scholars offer differing scenarios for this but agree on two main points: Jesus will return and govern the earth with righteousness, and there will be a time of judgment and a reconfiguration of the creation.

Some of earth's terrain may be retained in that new kingdom, but in an enhanced form—no longer groaning under the burden of sin. I hope so. God, who is love, pronounced the original creation good. From what we've experienced of love, we can expect God to renew that creation rather than destroy it. (There are a lot of places here on earth I'd like to explore, like the little roads in Oregon's forests that we're always going to take but never find the time for.) At the return of Jesus Christ the earth will be healed from wounds that sin and ignorance have inflicted. These wounds include cultural clutter, moral pollution, and environmental degradation.

"The heavens declare the glory of God," said the Psalmist (Ps. 19:1, KJV). Now on starry nights we gaze in wonder at the panorama of the heavens that astronomers observe more completely. Gadgets for amateurs are featured in magazines for devotees of stargazing. Other scientists and hobbyists look down rather than up, using increased magnification to examine inner material substance. But with all our instrumentation we've barely begun to enter into the mysteries of cosmic reality. One day we'll be equipped more fully to understand and enjoy them.

THE INHABITANTS OF HEAVEN

Whoever heads for unexplored territory wants to learn about the inhabitants. Though there is scant factual knowledge about the inhabitants of heaven, a list of potential candidates would have to include the following:

- Angels
- The church celestial
- Animals
- Extraterrestrials

Angels. We start by pondering heaven's natives, the angels. Angelic visitors have been reliably reported in the Bible. They have appeared, often in human form, on significant occasions, such as the call of Abraham, the visions of prophets, and the birth, life, and resurrection of Jesus. The presence of angels has been reported periodically by people since Bible times as well. I'm skeptical of some of these reports, especially when they're media-hyped, but others have the ring of truth.

Even though I've always accepted the biblical revelation of angels, I once found it hard to believe in angels in any physical sense. But that changed. I came to consider them spiritual beings, messengers of God living on a different plane of materiality. I'll narrate my route to this belief.

As a young scholar with a questing mind, the word *angel* seemed then a prescientific label for a benign quality, a virtue, or perhaps a spiritual force. I assumed that ideas reach a higher plane of reality than do things. In retrospect, my assumption arose from uncritically accepting a body/soul dualism. I didn't consciously denigrate physical substance; indeed, I affirmed and relished God's created order. But I had accommodated to a culture of modernity that separated the scientific from the spiritual. If scientific analysis couldn't locate angels in the created world, no problem; I would locate them in a secure realm of transcendental ideas. The adjective *angelic* seemed more suited to our enlightened era when applied to discerning and compassionate persons than did the noun *angel* when applied to heavenly personages.

But gradually I came to realize that the universe is much wider than hitherto surveyed by my limited mental equipment. Even as an academic person I didn't *dwell* in the realm of ideas, but in the physical world, interacting with other persons and creatures. My wife and children routinely helped me "come down to earth." Humbling experiences, such as one narrated below, also helped overcome that artificial division between the spiritual and the material.

In the prologue to his Gospel, John tells us that in Jesus Christ the eternal Word was made flesh and dwelt among us. If God thus incarnates his presence, surely (I came to realize) we creatures are called to live out Truth, and not just to organize it into notions. And so, throwing aside Platonic blinders, I asked myself this question: Why reduce personal entities to impersonal qualities? We often personify things: we do so when, for example, we name a car Penelope or a tornado Andrew. And yet the reverse—the reduction of persons to objects (physical or mental things)—we rightly deem unethical behavior. It seems to me that reducing angels to ideas falls into that latter category. Logically, such reduction isn't necessary. Ideas arise through beings, not beings through ideas—at least for us creatures.

So, as I pondered what to make of angels, I decided that it's as credible to believe in angels as it is to believe in qualities called "angelic." *More* credible, in fact, when we consider that God created a universe with beings and other material stuff, and called it good. He didn't just toss a glossary of words into the abyss. Now, I know that we can't infer the existence of centaurs from stories about them. As far as I know, however, nobody uses *centaur* as an adjective: "She's such a *centauric* person!" Yes, people *do* use mythical creatures sometimes to depict personal characteristics: for example, "He's elfin." But are angels in a class with centaurs and elves? I think not. (Mythic creatures serve as cultural pointers to realities lurking beyond ordinary perception.) The testimony about angels existing as beings and not merely subjects in mythic stories merits thoughtful respect. Angels are credible, if not easily explained in terms familiar to us.

So I now believe that angels are spiritual beings on a different dimension of materiality, but capable of taking on human (or other) forms in order to serve as agents (messengers) of the Almighty. I like what Karl Barth said of angels: "They are creatures, and as such wholly under God. . . . [W]here the angel is, there God Himself is present."[3]

In his vision of heaven, John the Revelator "heard the voice of many angels, numbering thousands upon thousands, and ten thousand times ten thousand" (Rev. 5:11, NIV). I accept this vision as depicting real creatures, and not merely painting a vivid word picture for appropriate attitudes of praise to the Almighty. Finding out more about these natives of heaven seems pretty exciting to me now, even though I wonder how we'll converse and interact. The biblical record suggests that these agents of God will accommodate to us.

Our culture is less closed-minded about supernatural beings than it used to be. Witness the rather successful CBS program *Touched by an Angel,* the plethora of popular books available on the subject, and the angel museum at Beloit, Wisconsin, which features artistic portrayals over the centuries (including Oprah Winfrey's collection of black angels).[4] There are also specific niches relating to angels: you can find hundreds of Internet sites and books offering to help you communicate with your guardian angel, for example.

I'm wary of entrepreneurial approaches, but I'm glad that people in contemporary culture are no longer walled in by secularism. Postmodernity has freed folks to explore spirituality. In today's culture spirituality flourishes, sometimes with godly awe and creative imagination, at other times as ego-centered forms of pop psychology and self-help. It's a mixture of the benign and the malign. The rite of exorcism is being employed more frequently than it used to be, in churches liturgical as well as charismatic. Satanic cults surface in the news from time to time, and their bizarre and bloody rituals send shivers down the spines of God-fearing persons. Such malign happenings remind us that there is a "horde of hell" as well as a heavenly host.

The middle ground between God and Satan is also popular. Some contemporary-cultured neo-animists follow superstitious fetishes, even delving into crystals and magic potions; but more persons in postmodernity are caught up in the exuberance of uncertainty, and they relish a game of life that seems now to have only provisional ground rules and no eternal principles. Under the banner of tolerance one may accept angels as symbols of virtuous living or as real entities—one story is as good as another.

The eyes of faith, however, see beyond the shallowness, distortion, and cynicism of these turbulent times. The eyes of faith envision many persons in the West becoming alive once again to mystery and open to the supernatural claims of the Gospel. An interest in angels is a sign of such openness. In the Greco-Roman era Christianity reached thousands within various nature religions who found life's mystery more fully revealed in Jesus Christ, who became God's Word of hope to them, became "good news." In evangelist Billy Graham's book about angels, he writes that believers should be more open to these messengers of the Lord, especially inasmuch as our nonbelieving culture has demonstrated a tragic fascination with the demonic spirits.[5] I honor Graham's discernment on this point. In an age of easy spirituality we may be misled by evil spirits perching on our psyches and posing as divine messengers and truth-bearers. "Even Satan disguises himself as an angel of light," wrote the apostle Paul (2 Cor. 11:14).

We tend to be more open to angels as helpers than as bearers of God's truth. Actually, in the Bible angels have diverse functions. They're bringers of divine help, comfort, and encouragement, as with Hagar, Elijah, and Mary, for example. They also appear as messengers instructing prophets about God's will and as agents of God's wrath. There's a humorous story in Numbers (22:21–35) in which Balaam's donkey sees God's angel, sword in hand, blocking the road, and refuses to proceed, even when beaten. The donkey, it seems, is not as blinded by self-deception as is her master! In thinking about angels we're well advised to consider that they're *God's* agents. Knowledge of and obedience to divine will, not personal comfort, is why they're sent to us.

Does each of us have a guardian angel? It could be. Some people think so, including Peter Kreeft, who has written a thoughtful book about angels. He calls them "immaterial substances" and notes about them, "Matter can't move through matter but spirit can. . . . Angels can move as easily as thought."[6]

The Orthodox Church considers guardian angels important enough to include this interesting prayer among its devotional guides:

Angel of Christ, holy guardian and protector of my soul and body, forgive me of everything I have done to offend you every day, and protect me from all influence and temptation of the evil one. May I never offend God by my sin. Pray for me to the Lord, that He may make me worthy of the grace of the All-holy Trinity, and of the Most Blessed Theotokos, and of all the Saints. Amen.[7]

I've not met my celestial guardian—or if I have, I didn't realize it. But I must admit that on occasion I've been rescued from stupidity in ways that later seemed to be miraculous interventions. I recall the time we young parents took our infant son with us for an afternoon drive up a remote Washington mountain. On a rutty logging trail we became stranded when our car broke down. Stupidly, we had neglected to take food and water. Nothing for the baby. No clothing adequate for mountain chill. No blankets in the car. Desperate and frightened, we waited and prayed for help as chilling darkness crept across the mountain. Suddenly, along came two loggers in a pickup, heading to the valley for the weekend. They stopped and peered under the hood. One of them found some rusty wire nearby and fiddled with what they'd determined to be the faulty component in our little 1937 Ford. Just like that, the engine started! We drove down the mountain and the loggers went their way. When we got home to Everett the car promptly quit again, and it required repair by a local mechanic.

Was it luck—a temporary fix—or was it angels? Initially we thought it was luck; but in reflecting upon the incident, we concluded it might have been angels sent to answer the desperate prayers of a young couple who had irresponsibly put their baby and themselves in peril. Or, if the loggers weren't angels, perhaps God just kept the men up the mountain a bit longer on our behalf.

Why were our prayers answered and not those of other foolish folk stranded in the mountains and not rescued? Does God juggle the books? And why have other equally desperate prayers of ours not been answered? I don't know. I can only testify to what I've experienced of God's judgment and mercy. In heaven it will be good to meet the natives who on occasion have been God's messengers. My wife and I would enjoy meeting our logger-friends in heaven, whether they're natives or immigrants like ourselves! Perhaps angels can explain miracles, the problem of evil, and the continuity/discontinuity of divine actions. Or come to think of it, maybe not: they may be baffled, too.

The church celestial. Our fellow human beings constitute the second group of heavenly inhabitants. I tend to think first of my family circle—my father gone from this earth for more than sixty years, my mother for nearly forty, my sister for seven. I wonder about other relatives, and about friends and neighbors recently deceased. Like a newly arrived immigrant excited to have landed in a new and better country, I would particularly anticipate meeting people who have arrived in heaven before me. I think of caring persons such as Mother Teresa, world shakers such as Abraham and Sarah, Moses, the apostle Paul, and Augustine, martyrs such as Perpetua, Justin, Mary Dyer, and Dietrich Bonhoeffer. I'll keep my eyes open for gifted leaders: Patrick, John Calvin, Menno Simons, George Fox, John Wesley, Isaac Newton, Martin Luther King Jr., and a host of others, including William Booth of the Salvation Army—that incorrigible optimist about God's power to redeem fallen humanity. I weep each time I read Vachel Lindsay's powerful poem of tribute, "General William Booth Enters into Heaven" (which is included in its entirety in Appendix B). It reminds me that an unfailing sign of the kingdom is that the poor receive the Gospel. Heaven will reveal the results of those who brought the good news to them. Perhaps you remember some of the lines:

> *Booth led boldly with his big bass drum—*
> *(Are you washed in the blood of the lamb?)*
> *The Saints smiled gravely and they said: "He's come."*

And, accompanied by sweet flute music, this poignant picture of God upon the throne:

> *Jesus came from out the court-house door,*
> *Stretched his hands above the passing poor.*
> *Booth saw not, but led his queer ones there*
> *Round and round the mighty court-house square.*
> *Yet in an instant all that blear review*

Marched on spotless, clad in raiment new.
The lame were straightened, withered limbs uncurled
And blind eyes opened on a new, sweet world.[8]

Heaven is much more than a family reunion, however, or a chance to meet particular saints. It's not a celebrity bash. Over the millennia billions of folks have died and gone to heaven. They have arrived from every tribe and tongue and people and nation as far back in time as the beginning of human history. Responding by faith to the Light within, they're enjoying eternal life in heaven. I envision considerable cultural shock at meeting folks from long ago, whose experiences on earth were so different than our own have been. Perhaps some of those ancients will be able to answer some questions for me—particularly questions about biblical personages and times. I would be interested to learn, for example, if Naomi saw Ruth again, and the courtly Boaz. I'd like to know whether Joshua met up with some of the innocents of Jericho whom he slaughtered—"collateral damage" is today's euphemism for those victims—and how that meeting went. I could use some help learning the difference between God's perfect and permitted will from those who've wrestled with that issue through the ages. This would be more instructive than discovering how a blare of trumpets could knock down walls, though I'd be glad to learn those technicalities, too.

What about those nameless ones from the dawn of time whose memory has been erased from history? How might one relate to people who never imagined, let alone drove, an automobile? How might one converse with illiterate hunters and gatherers from ancient times, persons who never used a computer or a telephone, who never saw, let alone read, a book? Well, if they could carve pictures on cave walls and, wailing with grief, bury their dead with food and prayers for the journey to the next world, surely we'll be able to find some things in common: hope, of course, but also curiosity, creativity, courage, a conscience to know right from wrong, a yearning to love and to be loved, a quest for the universe to make sense, and awe before the Creator.

Skill in surfing the Internet isn't the highest indicator of intelligence. A thousand years from now our present technology, unearthed by archeologists for public viewing, may seem as crude to earth's inhabitants then as stone axes seem to us now—that is, if earthlings don't destroy themselves or the earth sooner. It's wisdom that counts most, not knowledge. A lot of wisdom has been handed down to us over thousands of years, some in ancient Scriptures, some in oral traditions, some in art and artifacts. Heaven preserves that wisdom.

I believe that people are now in heaven, not in some sort of limbo waiting for termination of earthly affairs. Given the relativity of time, in relation to us they're already enjoying Jerusalem the Golden. They're ahead of us in understanding, too, and their presence is less circumscribed than ours. Sometimes we shiver with intimations of them hovering around us. The writer of the book of Hebrews refers to them as "a cloud of witnesses" (Heb. 12:1). They watch how we do our laps in the relay race of life. When I become discouraged, I like to picture my deceased friends cheering me on! Or when I wake up in the night with a solution for some nagging problem, it occurs to me that one of them has been kibitzing over my shoulder, empathetically nudging me with hints on the subject. They're with us, mind touching mind, spirit touching spirit, and one day, thank God, hand touching hand!

The animals. There's another class of inhabitants to consider: the animals. "The creatures great and small, the Lord God loves them all"—that's how the song goes. I confess perplexity on this matter. Although created by God, the creatures are of a lower order than we are, certain activists to the contrary notwithstanding. The early church leaders assumed that animals lacked rationality and therefore wouldn't be resurrected. I wouldn't put it that way, although the conclusion—no resurrection—may well be correct. The higher animals may not *know* that they know, but they do figure things out in their brains, and they exhibit emotional responses for getting it right or getting it wrong.

In any case, we've been charged with their oversight; we're their mentors, as it were. Human beings are central to God's care of the earth. We're not interlopers in nature. We *belong*. If God has covenanted with whales and chipmunks and eagles and slugs to be intelligent stewards of the earth, we've found no evidence for it or record of it. So species immortality would seem to be the case for animals and plants, in contrast to the individual resurrection offered humanity through God's grace.

This bothers me a bit, for I've had several dogs I'd like to see again, and a horse—Eagle was his name—I'd really love to ride once more across an Idaho pasture on a bright Saturday morning. Islamic literature supports a view that if we want specific animals in heaven we can have them. Presto, just like that. How intriguing! Well, maybe . . . maybe not.

The "peaceable kingdom" vision of Isaiah, captured on canvas by the early American artist Edward Hicks, shows animals living in harmony, not devouring each other. Hicks may have intended the image to be symbolic—but is it *merely* symbolic? If the peaceable kingdom is more than a metaphor for redeemed humanity, the food chain may have to be drastically reconstructed. And why not? God has made drastic changes before—for example, wiping out the dinosaurs with an asteroid. Other species may disappear, too, either as victims of civilization or natural catastrophes, or when judged by God to be unsuitable to a changed biosphere.

And perhaps—who knows?—God may breathe his spirit into creatures we know now, and some we don't know yet, and give them the gift of personal immortality. The earth is the Lord's, in all its fullness. A longtime Alaskan friend and consultant on Arctic flora and fauna, William R. "Bob" Uhl, observes that if, as we believe, heaven is a place of perfection, "God would have it well populated with animals for no other reason than to share in the fellowship of the relationships that have developed between the different individuals of His creation." Bob Uhl judges that a person's love for a horse or a dog might well be honored by a loving Creator, and that this fellowship might encompass "wild" animals, "whose majestic existence requires no keeper or caretaker other than their Creator." "Fellowship," he concludes, "that's the name of the game; what Creator could resist the opportunity to share in fellowship with all the remarkable aspects of His creation and their relationships to each other?"[9] I share Bob's hopes.

Yes, Isaiah's messianic "peaceable kingdom" poem may be largely symbolic, but again, the biblical hope is for a renewed creation, not just an improved social order within the present one. Isaiah wrote:

> The wolf will live with the lamb, the leopard will lie down with the goat, the calf and the lion and the yearling together; and a little child will lead them. The cow will feed with the bear, their young will lie down together, and the lion will eat straw like the ox. The infant will play near the hole of the cobra, and the young child put his hand into the viper's nest. They will neither harm nor destroy on all my holy mountain, for the earth will be full of the knowledge of the LORD as the waters cover the sea. In that day the Root of Jesse will stand as a banner for the peoples; the nations will rally to him, and his place of rest will be glorious. (Isaiah 11:6–10, NIV)

Extraterrestrials. What about other intelligent beings in the cosmos? Some people believe that from time to time aliens contact, or even abduct, earthlings. I'm not convinced that this happens. I'm also skeptical about the extraterrestrial nature of reported UFOs. I could be wrong, of course. But *if there are* inhabitants in some of God's other worlds, so be it. They aren't natives of heaven, though, as the angels are; that much we know. Rather, they—if they exist—are immigrants like us, just earlier or later in arriving. Such other intelligent beings might need redemption, too, or it might be that they haven't spoiled their garden as we *Homo sapiens* have done.

Ian Barbour believes that most scientists are open to the possibility of life in other galaxies, and he warns us against anthropocentrism, cautioning that other beings may be superior to us. He reminds us that "even on our planet the work of the *Logos,* the Eternal Word, was not confined to its self-expression in Christ. If that Word is active in continuing creation throughout the cosmos, we can assume that it will also have revealed itself as the power of redemption at other points in space and time."[10]

Finding other peoples in the cosmos, whether they're smarter or dumber, more or less advanced, standing two or ten feet tall, wouldn't diminish my faith. Actually, it would increase it. Losing God as a tribal deity, as we did ages ago, may have dented human egos for a while, but it certainly has enhanced human understanding of the Divine. Similarly, acknowledging God to be sovereign over the whole earth instead of a super-regent for the Roman empire (or the British, or the Aztec, or the Bantu, or the American, or the Chinese empire) obviously has been a step up for humanity. Perceiving God to be sovereign over a cosmos containing billions of galaxies, each with billions of stars and their planets, further enhances, or should enhance, God's stature in our minds. Relinquishing the theory that the earth is the center of the universe may have dashed human pride, but it sure enlarged our understanding of the universe and enhanced the stature of the Almighty! How much more awe-inspiring to know that the God whom we worship is sovereign over the whole creation (not just the atmosphere above us), including that elusive nine-tenths of the cosmos that we haven't the capacity to taste, smell, see, hear, or touch—yet.

SIX

What Sort of Persons Will We Be?

I want to know Christ and the power of his resurrection and the sharing of his sufferings by becoming like him in his death, if somehow I may attain the resurrection from the dead.[1]

—*Paul of Tarsus*

Shall that very flesh, which the Divine Creator formed with His own hands, which He set over all the works of His hand, to dwell amongst, to enjoy, and to rule them . . . whose sufferings for Himself He deems precious, shall that flesh . . . not rise again? God forbid! God forbid![2]

—*Tertullian of Carthage*

The glorified body is not a different body, but a different form of the same body.[3]

—*Thomas C. Oden*

SPIRITUAL BODIES

Paul of Tarsus, Tertullian of Carthage, and Oden of Drew University speak for the Christian community of faith across the centuries in the above epigraphs. This is foundational Christian doctrine: in raising Jesus from the dead God demonstrated a power sufficient to resurrect our bodies, too. In his resurrected body Jesus talked with the disciples and shared food with them, and yet he disappeared from their sight. Apparently Jesus could accommodate to earthly dimensions and also transcend them. The ascension that followed several weeks of appearances signified that such transcendence was the norm—at least until, as he said, "I will not leave you orphaned; I am coming to you" (John 14:18). He left the believers' sphere of reality so that the Spirit could extend divine presence more fully.

So by analogy we surmise that our resurrection bodies retain self-conscious identities and recognizable configurations but possess greater capabilities than our present earthly bodies. These new capabilities will surely include greater dimensional mobility. On earth we move within the three spatial dimensions that for purposes of measurement and control we designate as *length, width,* and *depth.* Physical mobility occurs linearly within the fourth dimension, *time,* although mental and spiritual mobility are less restricted to clock time.

Consider, for example, a basketball player. At six-foot-eight he can extend the *length* of his vertical line by leaping, but only by a few feet. Gravity pulls him down. He can try to block an opponent, but only to the *width* of his torso and relative to the *timing* of the other. If an opponent tries to drive *through* him, it won't work. Though the opponent might swivel around him, he can't penetrate through him. If he tries, the aggressor gets a charging foul and the defender bruised ribs. Our technology, of course, has greatly increased human mobility. We can go farther, range wider, probe deeper, and extend timelines farther than did our ancestors— but still within boundaries set by the four dimensions.

It seems credible to anticipate that resurrection bodies will achieve greatly increased mobility within space/time properties of a transformed universe. New dimensions will also be matched by better brains and heightened sensory capacities. Currently we perceive the world through five senses: seeing, hearing, tasting, smelling, and touching. Through these "messengers of God" we access reality—although unevenly.[4] (Dogs, for example, are better equipped to use the sense of smell than are their human companions.) In addition to the heightening of present senses, is it credible to anticipate that in heaven our senses may number many more than five? I believe so. A case might be made for a heightened "sixth sense"—intuition—that would obviate need for enhanced or additional sensory modes of knowing and communicating. Because God blessed the material creation and through Christ's resurrection affirmed the value of our bodies, it seems reasonable to consider that in heaven all ways of knowing, sensing, reasoning, and intuiting will be enhanced. It has been observed that a tiny minority of persons experience *synesthesia*. For them sensory experiences don't stay discrete but merge—for example, the brain puts colors to musical scores, or musical tones to scenic vistas, or taste to touch. The effect can be soothing, awe-inspiring, and/or confusing! Might synesthesia offer a clue to a heightened sensory potential for persons in heaven?

As noted in an earlier chapter, scientists calculate that we're in contact with only a tenth of *present* cosmic reality. They also posit as many as eleven dimensions. What might a basketball game in heaven be like if played within *eleven* dimensions instead of four, and if players could access strategy through a few more senses? To envision such a game we would need to invest with new meanings words such as *in, out, up, down, beside, across,* and *through.* Additionally, we would need to imagine time not as an arrow but as tide-driven waves rising, cresting, and surging along an immense and variegated shore. Or as light radiantly dispelling darkness at every opening. How might we compare the two games, the heavenly and the earthly? Like chess to tic-tac-toe, perhaps? Like ice-dancing to hopscotch?

From the beginning, the creeds of Christendom have stated forthrightly, "I believe in the resurrection of the body." That it's to be a spiritual body and not a resuscitated one is clearly taught in the New Testament and affirmed by the earliest Christian apologists. A definitive biblical passage on this issue comes from Paul in 1 Corinthians 15:35–57. This is part of what Paul wrote in that first-century letter:

> So it is with the resurrection of the dead. What is sown is perishable, what is raised is imperishable. It is sown in dishonor, it is raised in glory. It is sown in weakness, it is raised in power. It is sown a physical body, it is raised a spiritual body. If there is a physical body, there is also a spiritual body. (vv. 42–44)

Skeptics of bodily resurrection consider "spiritual body" an oxymoron. If God is spirit, and we become spirits, then how can we have bodies? They assume that what the disciples saw was an apparition of Jesus, produced by the charisma of his personality and the trauma of his death. If these skeptics are theists, they assume that spiritual renewal in this life and immortality in the mind of God in the next constitute the meaning of Jesus' resurrection, that "spirit" is ethereal and nebulous. If they're nonbelievers, they likely assume that early Christians made up the story of the resurrection to compensate for Jesus' failure to bring about the promised kingdom or that a hero's saga got embellished over time.

Here's my response to the skeptics. God is Creator, and we are his creatures. As beings created in the divine image, we're constituted as body, mind (in the sense of *psyche,* or soul), and spirit. Much of this life focuses upon the first two aspects of being; and rightly so, for there's a mystery about the body and that elusive part of it, mind, that exceeds material or chemical analysis of the nervous system. Mind can't be discovered by the use of magnetic brain scans. Ian Barbour rightly states that the Bible "looks on body, mind, and spirit as aspects of a personal unity." He clears up misunderstandings about Paul's contrast between "flesh and spirit" to show that sinful nature lies in the will, not in the body.[5]

J. A. Schep, an Australian Bible scholar, concurs with Barbour. Schep analyzes how the word *flesh* is used in the Bible—sometimes as a synonym for evil (for example, "heart of stone" or "sinful flesh") and other times as a synonym for weakness and finiteness. He shows that the physical body is understood as a good creation, honored of God and redeemed through Christ. Schep finds intimations of physical resurrection in Old Testament accounts such as the translation of Enoch and Elijah, descriptions of Yahweh's power to bring up the dead from Sheol, Job's assurance of justice beyond death, and prophetic predictions (for example, Daniel 2). He finds affirmations of physical resurrection throughout the New Testament. In discussing a controversial passage, 1 Corinthians 15 ("flesh and blood cannot inherit the kingdom of God," v. 50), Schep also insists that Paul refers to corrupt human nature, not to a nonembodied state of existence. He believes that Jesus didn't abandon his flesh-body at the ascension, and that this constitutes a pattern for believers.[6]

Jesus' incarnation and his resurrection appearances testify that God considers physical things, including sentient bodies, to be good. Sin resides in the will and not in the body. Redemption is a process of bringing human creation to its intended holiness.

Deep at the center of our being we intuit this pattern of embodied spirituality witnessed by Scripture and confirmed by Jesus' resurrection. Within each of us is a feeling for eternity, an understanding that we're spirit, encompassing body and mind (or soul). Belief in the resurrection presupposes a divine creation. God created all life, including human beings. Creation is a continuing process. Re-creation in the cosmos can and does occur. Human redemption, as well as human resurrection, is part of God's creative action. However vaguely or imperfectly we express it, people yearn for this wholeness. We cling to this faith stubbornly, against skeptics, repudiating voices of despair. We demonstrate a yearning to be fully human, to be spiritual beings. We refuse to ground the music of the human spirit in a silent universe.

The Word of creation and the Word of redemption confirm that a person is no less God's creature for being fitted with a spiritual, as opposed to an unspiritual (or natural), body.

We affirm that God creates us anew. What might this spiritual body "look" like? Let's put it another way: What will our *whole person* be like, when spirit is fully the context for body and mind? It's hard to perceive, isn't it? Religious speculators of an earlier era pictured spiritual bodies as benign, pale-faced, angelic figures garbed in white robes and sporting wings. Popular science fiction pictures extraterrestrials as small, bug-eyed, big-headed creatures sporting antennae.

This is what we *can* say. We're creatures, and we'll remain so, measured against the pattern of our creation—a pattern that ought to be observed carefully. Irenaeus of Lyons, writing against "spiritualizers" in the second century, affirmed the full humanity of Christ and the resurrection of real persons against Gnostics who demeaned the body. "Since men are real, they must have a real existence, not passing away into things which are not, but advancing among things that are."[7] A twentieth-century philosopher, D. Elton Trueblood, held similar concerns about over-spiritualizing heavenly existence. He wrote: "The resurrection faith is that we shall have concrete ways of knowing one another and that we are not to be dissolved into a general pool of spirituality."[8] A contemporary scholar concurs in respect to holistic personhood, but he warns against focusing too fully upon physicality. Ray S. Anderson of Fuller Seminary writes: "In Christian anthropology, human nature is not defined ultimately by tracing humanity back to its origins, nor by explaining humanity in terms of its existence under the conditions of sin. Rather human nature is life experienced as a personal body/soul unity, inspired and empowered by the Spirit of God."[9]

As creatures we have limits to our powers to know and to act. We experience boundaries within which life is contained and which distinguish us from other beings and from other entities. This is true for us on earth and will be true for us in heaven. As children we early learn about such boundaries. We discover that we can't fly like birds, although some of us certainly tried! We can't run as fast as bears, nor jump as high, proportionately, as grasshoppers. We can't be two places at once, or work without rest. I expect our heavenly bodies to exist within boundaries, too—although different ones. (Could walking through the woods include walking *through* the trees?) Knowing the present boundaries God has assigned us, isn't it reasonable to infer that in heaven we can't do everything we please? Don't envision the next life as one hedonistic binge! Being close to our Creator, and freed from sin's drag, however, we should be able to think more clearly and (with enhanced capabilities) to engage our reconstructed bodies in activities more wisely and happily. We should expect more fully to love our fellow citizens in heaven, and to love God with all our strength and mind and heart. To know God "face to face" instead of through a glass darkly is how Paul puts it (1 Cor. 13:12, KJV). I like that imagery!

Spirit and body aren't contradictories. Spirit exists with mental capacity and in some structural form. By analogy from Jesus' resurrected body, our own bodies will be not less but greater than before. A plant isn't less than the seed from which it sprang; it's greater. From the death of seed comes the life of the whole plant. To repeat what Paul said: "What is sown is perishable, what is raised is imperishable. . . . [I]t is raised in glory!" (1 Cor. 15:42).

CHANGES TO ANTICIPATE

Moving from an earthly to a heavenly existence "embodies" continuity as well as discontinuity. We've talked about some continuities, concluding, for example, that our resurrection selves will retain both physicality and self-conscious identity. What, now, are some of the *dis*continuities that we might anticipate? I suggest the following changes.

Anticipate probable physical changes. Through the ages and within different cultures people have believed that in heaven our bodies will be made whole. From what all religious traditions teach about God's evident concern for persons, we won't be look-alike robots fashioned upon an angelic template, but we'll be restored from impairment and given bodies fit, suitable, and uniquely our own.

Augustine used a striking metaphor to envision change: "What has been dissolved into dust or ashes, or returned to the basic elements, will be reconstituted by God, not tissue by tissue, hair by hair, but like an artist who restores from melted metal a statue as it had been."[10] For this North African philosopher, spiritual body indicated new-creation wholeness—a freedom from blemish, deformity, and, more importantly, the corruption of sin. Augustine puzzled over when life begins in the womb ("I do not know that any man can answer it") and about which aborted fetuses would be in heaven (musing that some seed doesn't germinate). However, he confidently expected defective bodies to be made whole, conjoined twins to be restored to "normal physiognomy," and babies to reach maturity.[11]

The hope of recovered physical wholeness understandably is strong among persons of advanced age and infirmity, as depicted in the following prayer:

A GARDEN WOULD BE NICE

Lord, I heard the doctor tell my daughter it's hospice time.
So before my mind gets dopey I must consider my death.
Not who gets the silverware but what happens to me.
Is it too much, Jesus, to be resurrected to about twenty-five?
Firm-bodied; not flabby, hunched and cancer-scarred?
And when I die will John hold me in his arms again
and say, sweetheart, you are so beautiful?
Am I just a foolish old woman to expect this?
By the way, Lord, I don't need a mansion,
but a flower garden would be nice. Thanks.[12]

PRAYERS AT TWILIGHT

I take great comfort in the hope that in heaven I'll continue to be me! I'll take whatever form God selects, and won't quibble if I don't regain a full head of hair. (Maybe hair won't even be a feature of the resurrected body, as resculpted by the Lord.)

Anticipate probable mental changes. We'll not be computerized robots in heaven; I'm sure of that. Our minds will vary in interest and aptitude, as they do now. Mathematically inclined persons should continue to enjoy number-crunching and will find ways to turn formulae into engineering projects. Likewise, I assume that literary persons will continue to be interested in verbal expressions and will find ways to employ words creatively. Professors will do research and teach. What libraries will be like depends upon what sort of bodies we have, what sort of sensory equipment we possess, and how knowledge is archived. Artists, poets, and musicians will express beauty in creative ways, using materials available in new and fascinating forms.

However configured intellectually, our minds will be free from sinful rationalizations. We will no longer be pressured by greed to pander to debased instincts, no longer tempted to yield principle to expediency. What a wonderful liberation! Deceitful hype will be out, of course: for heaven is out of bounds to liars. This will release lots of misspent energy. As God renews the earth and the rest of the cosmos, there will be plenty of opportunity—some sort of space/time reality—to use enhanced aptitudes and skills. It seems reasonable to assume that personality types will continue— that is, some of us will be shy and others outgoing, some aggressive and others passive. But ego-trips and posturing will be out. We will gladly learn from and respect others.

Anticipate probable spiritual changes. The Bible teaches that persons must be made holy to stand before the Lord in the heavenly life. *Sanctification* is the theological term for God's redemptive work in doing this. Sanctification is accomplished in our earthly life as God baptizes penitent sinners with the Holy Spirit. God's baptizing fire first frees us from the burden of guilt and then purifies the heart (our motives) and releases us from the grip of sin. The inclusive theological term for this transformation is *justification*. This term encompasses both pardoning for sins committed and cleansing from the inner sinful disposition. Often the term *justification* is used to connote God's forgiveness, and *sanctification* to connote God's actions that bring persons to holiness of heart and life. Sometimes the former term signifies *imputed* righteousness and the latter term *imparted* righteousness. In the biblical account of how sin entered and marred the world, our human ancestors, Adam and Eve, were created with freedom and with both the power not to sin and the power to sin. Beguiled by Satan, the tempter, they lost the power not to sin in what we call "the Fall." Redemption restores the power not to sin. Theologians argue over how far this process progresses in earthly life. They generally agree, though, that it's completed after death. This redemptive completion is called *glorification*. Glorification provides human immortality without the will or power to sin.

This moral boundary offers human freedom within the limits of God's authority. Early theologians used catchy Latin phrases to describe the sequence.[13] In Eden: *posse non peccare et posse peccare* (able not to sin and able to sin); after the Fall: *posse peccare* (able to sin). In the sanctified state: *posse non peccare et posse peccare* (able not to sin and able to sin); in heaven: *posse non peccare* (able not to sin). A seventeenth-century Reformed theologian, Johannes Wollebius, expressed it this way: "In the state of innocence man was able not to sin; in the state of glory he will not be able to sin."[14]

Freed from the guilt and power of sin, in the next life we come before the Lord as renewed and spiritually completed persons, ready for immortal heavenly experiences. Without sin to corrupt and destroy, we can handle enhanced sensory perceptions, we can make judgments from a cleansed mind, and we can express our emotions from clarified intuitions. Richard Baxter, a seventeenth-century writer, believed that we shall be spiritually receptive in a direct, intuitive way. He wrote: "We shall then have enlightened understandings without Scripture, and be governed without a written law; for the Lord will perfect his law in our hearts, and we shall be all perfectly taught of God."[15]

Anticipate probable character changes. In heaven how will we cope with earthly memories, some of which bring regret, sorrow, and remorse? In this life, humility before God enables us to understand ourselves and others (including how we may have sinned against them). Accepting first divine judgment and then divine grace, we're lifted from the slough of remorse to stride forward with strengthened character to the city of God. In heaven all memories, good and bad, will be woven into one's personal redemptive story, like a prelude to a fuller story of life with God in company with redeemed humanity, in a recreated cosmos.

In heaven we will use heightened energy and enhanced mobility constructively within the boundaries of the good, the true, and the beautiful. In that future heavenly state, we can't and won't corrupt the world, or be ourselves corrupted by demonic forces. We can't and won't debase our neighbors. We can and will achieve new understanding of the world(s) outside and within us. We can and will handle maturity unmarred by selfishness and uncrushed by adversity. We can and will become co-creators with Christ! His resurrection appearances offer a glimpse into a mode of existence transcending present spatial limits. We will exist within boundaries of knowledge and power—in that sense finite—but we will also be immortal.

Will we be preserved from stupidity? Well, yes and no. We will be spared stupidity arising from flawed character but not spared completely from errors in judgment, because our knowledge and power won't be absolute. We will remain creatures under the domain of the Creator. But we will be preserved from evil and from life-threatening danger.

Without evil will life lose its zest? Not for creatures blessed by the Almighty! How could we not be energized and greatly liberated for creativity when sin and guilt are replaced by holiness and joy? What a wonder, that God lets us share the glory!

SEVEN

Activity in Heaven

Who will taste death in the country of the One who lives
forever?[1]
—*Sharafuddin Maneri*

Death itself needs to be overcome, not just its sting
removed; human ultimate fulfillment requires a
temporally and spatially lived everlasting life.[2]
—*Miroslav Volf*

One question has bothered me about heaven. What will
people *do* in heaven? Spatial context and temporal sequence
are required in order for bodies (even spiritually cleansed ones) to
be mobile, to receive, expend, and conserve energy, to coexist with
things, and intelligently to set goals and accomplish personal and
social objectives. I believe that our heavenly bodies (which include
minds) will be active. We'll be more than information bytes
downloaded onto an eternal supercomputer. We will do things
like caring for our bodies, working, playing, socializing, sharing
affection, and worshiping.

I'll elaborate on heavenly activities later in this chapter, but first, how do I presume to know what we'll do in heaven? Well, there are reasonable grounds to extrapolate from the known to the unknown. Logical tests for any truth include *authority, consistency,* and *coherence.*

Let's look at the truth-test of *authority* first. I consider the Bible authoritative, though like everyone, I need the guidance of the Holy Spirit rightly to interpret and apply its message. Its teachings about a good creation and an effective redemption (through which we regain access to the "tree of life") imply a continuance of personal activity in heaven. Ubiquitous cultural expectations are less authoritative, although if God provides a witness in the hearts of people everywhere, as Paul wrote (Acts 14:17), then such cultural intimations of heavenly activity offer collateral weight. Projected activities in heaven are consistent with God's creative order, analogous to, although greater than, those experienced by us on earth. God reminds us, as he did by parading the animals before Job, that his realm includes creature activity, and that we should have more faith in divine sovereignty. "Is it by your wisdom," he asks, "that the hawk soars?" (Job 39:26).

Next we consider the logical truth-test of *consistency.* Physical activity in heaven is consistent with the teachings and example of Jesus. If Jesus' traits of integrity, justice, and love ought to characterize our discipleship in God's kingdom now, how much more in heaven! It takes bodies to effect qualities of character; minds that make moral decisions don't exist without them. Anticipating bodily activity in heaven is certainly consistent with and implied by the resurrection of Jesus. As for the truth-test of *coherence,* personal mental and physical activity in heaven makes sense in the overall scheme of things. It coheres with prospects of a rehabilitated material order.

The Bible forecasts certain heavenly activities, including offering praise to God and enjoying rest from struggle. The book of

Revelation celebrates the completion of the earthly pilgrimage with a song of Moses and the Lamb (chap. 15). The vision includes a huge crowd in heaven singing "Hallelujah! For the Lord our God the Almighty reigns!" (chap. 19). I'm grateful enough for God's redemption to spend considerable time singing my thanks, with tears of joy for the divine triumph over evil (including my own sins), but heavenly activity will be more than singing hymns. Weary and traumatized persons, upon entering heaven, may indeed need a long, unstressed rest. For a young mother of five who succumbed to AIDS, or a political hostage tortured to death, heaven may mean an angelic hand on a fevered brow or Jesus' arm about a tortured body. To all who arrive in heaven as victims of violence, the initial experience may well be simply to bask in the love of martyred saints who rest "in the bosom of Abraham." Richard Baxter expressed it well for all who have suffered greatly in this life: "We who have gone through the day of sadness, shall enjoy together that day of gladness," and "we shall then have joy without sorrow, and rest without weariness."[3]

A renewed and wholly righteous universe is not just a place of singing and rest, however. Even the greatest celebrations of release from troubles don't go on forever. To hallow the name of the Holy One of Israel means more than a feast, although this biblical metaphor is a great one! It's especially treasured by persons haunted in this life by the specter of starvation. But who wants a parade and a barbecue every day? Or who wants to sit in church constantly?

Can we take our clues from the Sabbath principle? Life dances to rhythm! Biblical Sabbath teachings extol a rhythm of routine and rest, with more of the former and less of the latter. After initial hymns of praise before God's throne, after the thunderous pealing of orchestras and brass bands and angel choirs singing "Glory to the Lamb!" after joyful reunions with loved ones and an introductory tour of the region of heaven assigned to us, what then?

What some people fear most of all about eternal life is boredom. Garth L. Hallett, a contemporary philosopher, suggests six reasons that we need not fear boredom in heaven. They are: timeless beatitude, heavenly continuation, indefinite progress, subjective timelessness, eternal youthfulness, and creative contentment. (In other words, assured of a healthy body and creative mind in a continuously peaceful environment, how could one become bored?) Hallett considers that the six "form a cumulative case" for envisioning qualitative values that can endure indefinitely and meaningfully. He acknowledges, however, that there may be other ways we can't think of now, and suggests that we should take our cues from the great mystics, who couldn't conceive of being bored with God in eternity.[4] Heaven, after all, is God's gift, and from what believers have experienced of the Creator's redeeming grace, that gift of eternal life will exceed expectations.

To help answer our questions about activity in heaven, let's consider what we do now, on earth. We do many things, so I'll group these diverse activities into categories. Here's a short list of activities, along with thoughts about how we might continue them in heaven (but in exponentially greater ways than on earth):

PHYSICAL MAINTENANCE

Basically, as earthly creatures we receive energy for our bodies from the sun. This occurs via photosynthesis, primarily through plants and secondarily through animal products consumed. Ingestion, elimination, and rest are elemental daily activities. The first maintenance chore—ingestion—is often a social occasion, whether as a family breakfast or as a restaurant dinner with friends. The second—elimination—occurs privately, behind the bathroom door. Scatological jokes, though quirky and boorish, constitute backhanded compliments to a vital bodily function that puts everyone on the same level. Elimination is the great equalizer!

A third maintenance activity, rest, is achieved through a mixture of private and public actions—private sleep in our beds at night, public naps on park benches or buses during the day, for example. "Sleeping together" has become a euphemism for sexual activity, but it certainly means far more. Sleeping together is part of a social rhythm that physically produces life and psychologically produces intimacy. Whatever the nature of the spiritual bodies we will have in heaven, they will continue to be energized by God's creation. If not derived directly or indirectly from the sun, our energy may derive from light itself.

Will we retain our digestive system? Maybe; maybe not. The resurrected Christ ate food with his disciples, but that could have been a this-worldly accommodation to validate his bodily resurrection to bewildered disciples (and our own resurrection to us). Will we be vegetarian? Isaiah's vision of the peaceable kingdom, noted in a previous chapter, certainly hints at an end of an *animal*-based food chain: "The cow and the bear shall graze, their young shall lie down together; and the lion shall eat straw like the ox" (Isa. 11:7). I'm inclined to interpret the vision a bit more symbolically, to signify a radical shift in the heavenly nature of animate life as it takes on new and enhanced material forms and symbiotic relationships. What is the food chain but a sequence of life out of death? In heaven, however, death has been defeated; life reigns.

It's difficult to foresee *how* our bodies might be sustained without those nutrient cycles that characterize our earthly life. Though we can only speculate about specifics, of one thing we may be confident: God the Creator remains—and will remain forever—our source of life. To reiterate a point: on earth God sustains human life by light—indirectly, through vegetable, animal, and mineral materiality. It seems reasonable, therefore, to suppose that in heaven God will sustain our life more directly through light, without intermediate energy sources. Significantly, Jesus Christ is called the *Light of the world*. To me this implies that material and spiritual energy are complementary aspects of God's life-sustaining power.

In this life we don't just *feed* our bodies. We care for them in other ways as well. We groom ourselves; we choose and wear suitable clothes; we build houses for shelter. Our tended lawns and flower gardens add aesthetic extensions to our selves. We exercise to sustain strength for our tasks. Early Christians speculated about whether mouths would be needed in heaven if we wouldn't be eating regular food. But they judged mouths in any case useful to sing praises to the Lord! What about the other body parts? Well, they thought that even though nonfunctional, our organs could remain as testimony to creation. They missed the point with that conclusion, though. Bodies decayed in the earth or eaten by sharks or cremated won't just be reassembled into original parts to be exhibited like stuffed animals in a museum. No. God who raised Jesus from the dead will provide us with *new* bodies, similar to his resurrection body, with personal identity intact. These bodies will be suitable to the terrain of heaven, mobile, and capable of intelligent communion with God, with the angels, with each other, and with all other created entities (whether sentient or not).

These new bodies should enable us to perform tasks as stewards of creation. Through the resurrection God brings humanity back to its original mandate. Eden revisited it is, indeed, but this time with a freedom effected by redemptive triumph over sin. Human minds require bodies with a central nervous system. Bodies come with brains. Minds don't exist without brains and bodies. Spiritual bodies are still bodies. Thinking, whether in the form of reasoning or praying, expends energy, and without healthy bodies mental, spiritual, and physical activities fail. So I surmise that people in heaven are not nebulous gas blobs floating about among the stars, but intelligent, self-conscious, beautiful creatures whose resurrection bodies act in ways resembling present modes, but at enhanced levels of power.

Presently, sleep offers us a feeling for eternity. Each day is a sort of forever. Sleep breaks lived time into sequenced segments, thus enriching life through memory and anticipation. We awake restored, to live fully in the present. Through sleep, and other forms of rest, we gain respite from the weight of continued conscious existence. Doesn't it make sense to assume some sort of heavenly equivalent to earthly rhythms of activity and rest? Without the burden of anxiety, and with greatly enhanced mental and physical capabilities, we can surely manage endlessness "one day at a time!"

Let's now consider how other earthly activities might continue in the afterlife.

WORK

Work is not just what people get paid to do. As distinguished from play, work is an instrumental good. It produces intrinsic social value. For example, the work of a farmer yields necessary food; that of a carpenter, useful shelter; that of a taxi driver, needed transportation services; that of a doctor, health care; that of an attorney, legal advice; that of a teacher, knowledge; and so on. Our present existence is sustained by a division of labor theoretically appropriate to individual skills and to social beings in community. We know, sadly, how inequitable that division is in a sin-cursed world! Some people labor hard to the benefit of others who labor little. Work as such, however, isn't a consequence of sin. Toil, yes—and, metaphorically, thorns; but not labor. In Eden humanity received a mandate to tend one of God's gardens—the earth. Thus to labor means to participate in a divinely ordered activity. In his visionary trek through heaven, Emanuel Swedenborg interviewed a botanist who was enraptured by the beautiful parks in heaven, and particularly in one of them by an overwhelming abundance of plants and flowers, which he was allowed to examine and care for.[5]

Empowered by God's spirit (and freed from sinful hindrances), our resurrected selves in heaven will have greatly increased abilities. Present earthly dimensions—height, breadth, depth—will be extended or supplemented. But if our persons will have changed (as from seed to stalk), so will the size of God's garden. It's reasonable to expect that our mandate for stewardship of Eden will continue in heaven, with the renovated cosmos our workplace, of which earth may continue to be part. We'll have things to do, the will and skill to do them, and the wisdom to work within God's sovereign purposes.

This cosmos (or another one) will include that uniquely human contribution to life on earth—the city. By "the city" I mean not just a place of urban living, but *civilization,* with its languages, its technologies, its governance, and its culture. On earth the physical city has often degenerated into a cesspool of iniquity marked by poverty at the center and greed at the periphery. Nature has suffered, too, because of sin in the city of man. But under truth-seeking minds, the city of God has come to earth at various levels of approximation. Nurtured by this vision of a righteous realm, the city of man has had intimations of a coming splendor. Civilization has brought health and safety. It has brought freedom from toil and provided creative enjoyment to millions of people. How much more, freed from the curse of sin, will civilization flourish! Heaven will provide for urban as well as pastoral living. It's that blend of divine and human creativity that John the Revelator captured in his vision of Eden and the New Jerusalem harmoniously joined.

Already the city of man explores its galaxy and sends its probes into outer space. Already the city has catalogued the human genome. Reaching further in and farther out, humanity is poised on the edge of incredible explorations. Scientific discoveries promise healthier and extended living for the inhabitants of the world, or at least for some of them. With the curse of sin gone and apocalypse past, surely human beings in heaven will become active stewards of the Lord in completing or extending the universe of things and ideas. Civilization is not old; it has barely begun!

PLAY

An old catechism asks this question: "What is the chief end of man?" and responds thus, "to glorify God and to enjoy him forever." Play is joyful activity; it's energy expended on unnecessary action. Play accents intrinsic over instrumental values. When we play, body, mind, and spirit unite in a way that betokens the wholeness of our resurrected experience in heaven. Play is an end in itself, and not a means toward another, although good ends (such as health and friendship) may result from playful activities.

During childhood years we play innocently, putting strength of body and mind and spirit into games without regard for whether the activity yields anything needed to sustain life. Trees and stones and mud puddles and grass and dogs and cats are, for children, things to enjoy. Adults, on the other hand, tend to be too overworked, too oppressed by poverty or by wealth, to recognize enjoyment. Oh, they play too, of course (though less innocently than do children)—tiddlywinks or golf, Scrabble or bridge, volleyball or tennis, pipe organ or guitar, parachuting or Parcheesi, crossword puzzles or mountain climbing. (It's a reliable creation that makes these activities possible. We can trust the ball to bounce off the wall or into the basket, or to cross the batter's plate in predictable ways. We can calculate odds in card games.) But in our affluent Western societies play and work get distorted: professionals get paid to play, whereas unpaid volunteers donate time and skill to work at building houses for the needy or teaching illiterate persons to read.

Jesus urged dour adults to put on happy faces and become like little children in order to participate in the kingdom. Don't fret over necessities, he insisted. In that message lies the implication that play echoes eternity, that the second Eden welcomes childlikeness and remains unmarred by "childish" selfishness.

Under optimum conditions play is sustained by an economic order that doesn't sap all human energy just to survive. And yet clearly, *many* conditions in human society are far from optimal! Sin heaps drudgery upon people, upon the rich burdened with too much of this world's goods, and upon the poor burdened with too little. Some professionals work eighty hours a week in *one* job, while some service workers labor eighty hours a week in *two* jobs. Absent the misery of poverty or wealth, freed from infirmity, restricted from petty jealousies and sinful pride, and with time on our hands, why shouldn't heaven be a wonderful place to play? We will all be, as Jesus said, "children of the resurrection" (Luke 20:36).

H. A. Williams illustrates the wholeness of resurrected persons this way: "When I play a game well, I have for that limited period of time an experience of the body's resurrection. For there is no hint of a dualism between mind and body with either of them trying to oppress or bully the other. I bring to the game my total undivided self."[6]

As children of the resurrection, guilt-free persons take each day as a gift. They're playful in the best sense of that word. As the old song goes, they "live for the day nor anxious be." Though remaining limited in strength and knowledge, in heaven persons redeemed by God's grace can surely experience each "day" as an eternity. On earth rhythms of life stave off monotony. How much more in heaven! With resurrection bodies, with a society free from sin, and within a liberated universe, enjoyment won't fade. It's the weight of sin that jades the spirit and wearies the body. Heaven, as Paul said, is "an eternal weight of glory" (2 Cor. 4:17). We won't get bored bearing that burden! The line between work and play is blurred whenever and wherever the burden of sin has been lifted. But that's okay. There really isn't much distinction between work and play when activities are offered in love to God and to others, when ends and means merge in a spiritual discipline, achieving and blending the classic aesthetic goals of life: the good, the true, and the beautiful.

PRODUCTION

All humans make things, whether we're working or playing. Some folks build bridges, others sew quilts; some write sonnets, others carve statues; some design airplanes, others construct software systems. Artists paint seascapes or weld junk into iron horses. Children build sandcastles. Adults construct barns and houses and skyscrapers and ships and airplanes. I make things—articles such as walking sticks and clocks—from wood gathered by beachcombing. We all use material stuff to create immaterial values.

Will there be opportunities in heaven to make things? Why not? If not these particular opportunities, then others beyond our capacity to imagine now will surely challenge our enhanced capabilities. When God stood back and looked at the creation and called it good, he blessed material substance. Just as the body is the temple of the Holy Spirit, so created things are blessed of God. In the divine image we share a creativity to design and make things. This penchant for creation will only be enhanced in heaven, not diminished.

SOCIAL INTERCHANGE

All of us spend time with other people. We talk at the grocery store or the coffee shop and as we pass each other on the street. We visit each other's homes and watch movies together. We correspond via e-mail. We take family trips and go out for dinner. We converse at work and play, and chat after worship. We kid each other and tell jokes. We share memories, especially good ones. We laugh at funny things that happen to us and to other people. We pet our cats and throw sticks for our dogs to fetch. We tell stories to our children and put on plays.

Sometimes socializing becomes an occasion for sin, as when we put other people down instead of laughing with them, compete unfairly in games or in business, turn casual friendships into exploitive abuse, betray our spouse by adultery, steal a neighbor's car or reputation. Social life can tear families apart as well as knit them together. Youth are especially vulnerable; easily exploited, they become trapped in a subculture foisted upon them by clever entrepreneurs. Busy adults are vulnerable, too, though. They succumb to assorted sins lurking within the workplace. They fall prey to pyramid schemes. As senior citizens they get ripped off by official-sounding "financial advisors." All of us have seen gossip among a friendly clique damage excluded outsiders, seen pride and covetousness destroy a friendship, seen broken covenants and hedged promises bring grief to families and nations, seen sin evidenced by snobbery and exploited trust.

John Calvin is remembered for espousing the work ethic, but perhaps he also should be noted for honoring the gifts of ordinary people. His doctrine of election was egalitarian—God alone determines social worth, not kings, caste, or culture. Calvin wrote about society as the body of Christ: "As Christ begins the glory of his body in this world with manifold diversity of gifts, and increases it by degrees, so also he will perfect it in heaven."[7]

With "clean hands and pure hearts"—better social skills—we will surely be able to enjoy each other more. We will be able to laugh at our stumbles and at funny situations that arise among creatures limited in understanding and skill. We will learn from our mistakes instead of wasting energy shielding the ego from the discovery (and criticism) of our goofs. In heaven nobody will have to prove worth by denigrating a neighbor, or ridiculing another person, or betraying a friend. Socializing in heaven won't involve trashing other people, but getting to know and enjoy one another. Protective psychological coverings won't be needed. Such masks and deceptions now infect worldly society. Who needs celebrities and groupies in heaven? In heaven *all* are "beautiful people." With a bit of angelic prodding I expect we will be able to improve our capacity for seeing people as God sees them rather than as earthly society has stereotyped them.

TRAVEL AND CULTURAL EXCHANGES

The tourist industry is an important economic enterprise in many places. Folks like to see how other people live, what they eat, how they dress, what their important structures look like, what they do for a living, and what kind of art they create. Currently some marginalized persons, such as the San (Bushmen) of Africa, have had to pander to tourists in order to survive—offering themselves as museum exhibits during the day and at night drowning their social dislocation in alcohol. Surely heaven will permit us to enjoy cultural exchanges without demeaning each other or having to pander to others. We will enjoy a wealth of artistic and social creativity. The earth is filled with interesting and beautiful places, natural and artificial, that we like to visit, whether we go to such natural wonders as the Oregon coast, the Bay of Fundy, the fjords of Norway, the outback of Australia, or the rainforest of Brazil, or to such human wonders as the Taj Mahal, Egypt's pyramids, the cathedrals of Europe, or Seattle's Space Needle.

In heaven, with uncounted galaxies to explore, some mode of safe and speedy travel would seem to be required! In some form light will probably provide the energy, more directly and efficiently than is presently the case. Humanity is highly mobile, and will continue to be. If you're like me, you've envied the birds their ability to ride heat thermals up steep mountain slopes, or to soar above cresting ocean waves. Our movements seem clumsy by comparison. In heaven we will share their grace. For now, though, we cherish our automobiles for their ability to take us sightseeing, and trains and ships and airplanes for carrying us to distant and exotic places. Our earth is filled with fascinating places! A lifetime isn't long enough to do more than experience a bit of it. The cosmos is so vast! An eternity won't be too long to explore the galaxies. For a starter, how about one planet a century, the Milky Way in a millennium?

AFFECTION

As a youngster I took a dim view of heaven whenever I heard folks talk about it. The experience of being draped with a white sheet as an angel for one Christmas pageant didn't help my receptivity to notions of an afterlife existence. Angels seemed sexless and dull. This notion was reinforced in my young mind when I heard a Bible story about how the liberal party of the times tried to trick Jesus. The Sadducees posed a legal tangle about a man who had been married to seven women. "Whose would she be in heaven?" they chortled. Obviously they sought to make the orthodox Jewish notion of heaven look silly. As on similar occasions, Jesus sprang the trap without getting caught. He replied, "The people of this age marry and are given in marriage. But those who are considered worthy of taking part in that age and in the resurrection from the dead will neither marry nor be given in marriage, and they can no longer die; for they are like the angels. They are God's children, since they are children of the resurrection" (Luke 20:34–36, NIV).

I didn't object to Jesus deftly eluding his detractors' trap. Indeed, I applauded it. But no marriage? Does this mean no sex? Many males think about sex quite often—many times a day, some psychologists have calculated, although how they know eludes me. In any case, as a young man I couldn't imagine that free sex occurred in heaven, nor do I think so now. If faithfulness to a spouse is a virtue on earth, then how much more in heaven! So I've pondered how the analogy of seed to stalk could apply in this matter.

Another of Paul's analogies, comparing this life to a tent and heavenly life to a mansion, is helpful. I've concluded that the most ecstatic orgasm ever experienced in a love-caressed marriage won't hold a candle to what touch and taste and smell and sight and sound will bring to "children of the resurrection," to persons sanctified and glorified by the Holy Spirit. I can imagine capacities for love-expressions in a magnitude of self-fulfilling powers only hinted at by earthly joys of sex and companionship. As my wife and I approach sixty years of marriage, we've discovered that even lacing fingers together on a walk along the seashore suffices to produce emotional power it would have taken considerably more passion to generate in younger years.

After passing through the tunnel of death can we walk about in God's garden, holding hands? Can we play golf at six-thirty on a summer morning? Or enjoy games of Scrabble on long winter evenings? I don't know about these specifics. But I have assurance about this question: Can we find ecstasy in heavenly companionship? Yes, we can and we will! And what we experience in intimacy can be shared on friendship levels with other mutually trusting persons. As Paul so aptly put it, "Love never fails" (1 Cor. 13:8, NIV).

WORSHIP

Perhaps I should have put worship first, because heaven is popularly perceived as a huge choir gathered around God's golden throne. Actually, that's a great picture. What a thrill to be in the presence of God the Creator and all the angels and inhabitants of heaven! To experience such unity with the Divine! As Paul said, "Now we see in a mirror dimly, but then we will see face to face. Now I know only in part; then I will know fully, even as I have been fully known" (1 Cor. 13:12). Moses reportedly had to wear a veil to face the brilliance of the Holy One. In worship we learn of God, translating knowledge into wisdom. If the fear of the Lord is the beginning of knowledge, how much more will that holy awe, purged of sin, yield a sanctified curiosity about God and the creation.

John Gilmore puts it this way:

> The knowledge of God, especially, will take priority over any other disciplines continued. Unlike the acquisition of the knowledge of God on earth, it will not be subject to erosion, exaggeration, and error. Because of a fuller and more accurate insight into the character of God, all other activities, occupations, and duties will reach the ideals cut short by sin in the Garden of Eden.[8]

If our ecstatic experiences of God in this life are any clue—the times when we weep with joy at the marvel of forgiveness, when we gaze in wonder at a waterfall, or laugh with joy at serendipitous awakenings to God's love—we can certainly expect worship in heaven to be grander than any worship service we've ever attended. Imagine thousands and thousands of us from every tongue and tribe and nation and people singing "Amazing Grace." Chills run down my spine just pondering it! Especially that final stanza added by John Rees: "When we've been there ten thousand years, bright shining as the sun, we've no less days to sing God's praise than when we'd first begun." In a chapter entitled "Occupations of the Redeemed in Heaven," a Bible expositor of a previous generation, Wilbur Smith, wrote, "The first great and continuous activity for the redeemed will be worship of the triune God." Other activities that Smith anticipated are service, fellowship, and learning.[9]

Earthly worship in one form or another includes proclaiming God's truth, having fellowship with one another, and serving others. Such is God's mandate for the church terrestrial. The church celestial may be similar, but with more focus on fellowship and service. Worship is more than hymns and prayers, more than contemplative ecstasy, more than a choir singing Handel's "Hallelujah" chorus. Worship means responding to the worth of God and the worth of God's creation.

At the top of the ladder of spiritual ascent we discover our true vocation: to be co-creators with Christ. To honor the worthiness of God we fulfill the Genesis account of our fashioning—we act as creatures made in the image of God. God has given to us the mandate to care for the earth and to do so righteously. Righteousness involves society ordered by the Lord—a theocracy, if you please. It involves sensing and expressing beauty. It also involves participation in the practical care of the creation.

In the next chapter we look at society in heaven, and in the following one the renewed cosmos. If we consider eternity only as endlessness, we miss its fullness, its larger dimensions. For time flows within eternity's banks, and its course should be envisioned as high and wide and deep, as in and out and through, not just as flat and narrow and long.

EIGHT

Society in Heaven

Finish then thy new creation, pure and spotless let us be;
let us see thy great salvation, perfectly restored in Thee.
Changed from glory into glory, 'til in heaven we take our
    place,
'til we cast our crowns before Thee, lost in wonder, love,
    and praise.
—*Charles Wesley*

I'D LIKE THAT!

Lord, I don't travel much anymore.
Went to the Columbia ice fields last year,
But most of the scenes I view now
are inside my head. Some are vivid,
like seeing that dirty trench near St. Lo,
the red blood spurting from my leg,
and that German boy's face—
before I blew it away. I never talk
to anyone about this, except you, Lord.
Maybe I'll meet that boy in heaven.

That would be okay. We'll recognize
and forgive each other, and maybe you
will give us constructive work to do
together, somewhere in the cosmos.
Yeah, I'd like that. . . .[1]
—*Prayers at Twilight*

By the word *society* I don't mean teas and celebrity pages of the
newspaper, nor do I refer to aggregate numbers. Newspapers
and statistics don't tell the whole story about community. In a
deeper sense *society* means people relating to one another in reasonably harmonious ways, doing together (whether from necessity
or from choice) what can't be done alone. People sort themselves,
or get sorted, into affinity groups for social interaction. The social
self makes whole the integral self. People discover who they are
through their participation with others—with families, work crews,
regional associations, and hobby groups. Aesthetic and ethical
predilections direct interest.

These relationships identify who one is. Legal covenants set
ground rules for such social interactions, and governments enforce
them. A good society provides sufficient cohesiveness for useful
interchange of goods and services. In a well-functioning society
people need and respect each other. They consent to be governed,
not only to avoid evil but also to maximize good for the individual
and the group. A well-functioning society enhances the common
good. A malfunctioning society diminishes it. Inept or corrupt government allows cabals of selfish individuals to exploit others, ren-
dering many citizens virtually powerless. Such social dysfunction is
an all-too-familiar pattern in history, and it's a feature of contemporary society. Sin has obviously badly infected the earthly city. How,
then, does heaven model a society purged of sin—the *good* society?

Consider again the prayer Jesus taught his disciples: "Thy will be done, on earth as it is in heaven." We infer from this that Jesus extolled a definitive and holy pattern for earth's people to follow. Thus for those who believe in God, heaven is more than a theoretical human construct, more than idealization of the possible, more than extrapolation from finite to infinite notions, more than someone's vision of an ideal world. Heaven is *real*, however elusive its formal and material configurations may be for us now.

Our minds find it difficult to grasp the "where-ness" of heaven, as noted in Chapter Two; and we also grapple with the "what-ness" of persons and their relationships in a resurrected state. Yet, as we saw in Chapter Six, all the evidence available to us suggests that in heaven we will do God's will *as embodied creatures,* as we're admonished to do on earth. Warren S. Brown strongly affirms this physicalist view of personhood. Human beings, he writes, "are what you see; there is not another invisible, non-material entity to be factored into the formula of understanding."[2] Such an affirmation of personhood enhances the reality of *relationships* and forecasts the *interactive* nature of heavenly society.

So the admonition for laudatory human actions bears an authoritative stamp. Heaven is where harmonious social order actually occurs. It's correct to say that we enjoy a bit of heaven on earth whenever and wherever love prevails and truth reigns. That bit of heaven isn't the whole, but it's a significant part. Heaven, then, serves as a model and guide for any interaction or social system in which God's will isn't yet in place. Heaven certainly does *not* model a society that makes idols of some folks and pariahs of others. It does *not* model a social system that fosters and rewards greed, selfishness, and hatred. Love, honesty, justice, and mercy are operational principles in heaven as they should be on earth, and as they will be when Christ returns to make it fully so.

It seems unlikely that, on reaching heaven, people automatically acquire perfect knowledge or wisdom; but at least, through redemptive grace, their hearts are purified of deceit, greed, selfishness, and duplicity. God gives them an inner disposition to make relationships work rightly, and empowers them to act on that disposition. People argue about whether social chaos arises from bad systems or bad people. William Penn observed that the best system of government fails if people are bad and the worst works if people are good. In heaven bad people can't sabotage the system. Neither can a degenerate social system frustrate good people or turn them cynical. If in this life redeemed people overcome limitations of knowledge to make the social order function reasonably well, how much more in the next? After all, believers look to their redeemer, Jesus, to lead the heavenly kingdom. In the vision of John the Revelator, Jesus is the "Lamb upon the throne" (Rev. 7:17). (What a powerful metaphor!) God provides in a heavenly ruler one who has suffered with and for us, has borne our sorrows, who laid down his life for our salvation. Our Messiah has entered fully the human condition, but without sin. Under the governance of the crucified and risen Lord, earthly society becomes the peaceable kingdom. The meek *do* inherit the earth.

People exploited by cruel or selfish persons or by a sin-infected social system find the hope of heaven reassuring. Those who pray for God's will to be done on earth are vindicated by the knowledge that although justice and goodness prevail *partially* in this life, they will prevail *fully* in the next. God is not mocked by sin; neither are those who fear him. Miroslav Volf puts it succinctly: "Without an afterlife, neither final justification nor the final social reconciliation is possible."[3] With the patriarch Abraham, persons of faith confidently ask their Maker, "Shall not the Judge of all the earth do what is just?" (Gen. 18:25). A strong hope of social equity sustains their social and political actions. They build for eternity, not for this era or that nation. Jesus, not Machiavelli, guides their ethical decisions. They resist using evil means to achieve good ends. They don't become disillusioned by setbacks, nor do they allow degenerate culture, corrupt politics, or collapsed civilizations to drive them to despair.

The wind of God blows away the smog of cynicism for people of faith. To use a phrase from the book of Hebrews, believers look forward "to the city that has foundations, whose architect and builder is God" (Heb. 11:10). They have seen the heavenly city shining at the world's horizon, and they follow Jesus toward its gates, holding in their hearts God's passport to the celestial city—the indwelling Holy Spirit. Such persons do God's will on earth; they're energized by hope and filled with joy. Their works of love and truth leaven the earthly city, making it an anteroom to heaven.

Building on the belief that heaven is an archetype for earth, let's now probe the mysteries of the divine realm that provides a model for what our earthly society should be.

SOCIAL ORDER IN HEAVEN

So what will heavenly society be like? Jesus spoke of the kingdom of God as a realm fulfilling limited earthly efforts at human community. Whenever and wherever society now is marked by justice and by goodness, it partakes of the heavenly kingdom. The biblical litany describing those gathered into heaven depicts a striking inclusiveness: "from every tribe and language and people and nation" (Rev. 5:9).

The kingdom of God is contrasted with the kingdom of man, which takes shape in circles of ethnic, political, and cultural affinity. These affinity groups—these "kingdoms"—historically bring order for a while, though often via bloody conquest and oppression, and by exclusion or debasement of others. Diversity of skills and tools drives humanity toward formation of increasingly larger social units, and toward interdependence of goods and services. These larger governing units offer sufficient freedom and economic stability for civilization to flourish creatively for a few centuries. Sooner or later, however, sins of pride, avarice, and greed fracture the system. Then anarchists destroy the good life at its creative edge and/or tyrants destroy it at its moral center. The social covenant shatters under violent attack. Nations destruct; empires fall; and finally an entire civilization collapses amid a debris of broken lives and shattered hopes. Such is the history of the human city: gradual evolution followed by violent collapse. But that isn't the end of the cycle. Human yearnings for a just and compassionate, inclusive human community arise out of the ashes, and a slow rebirth begins.

God won't let this cycle continue until the sun burns out and humanity disappears. He doesn't mock us in our quest for community. He isn't silent about evil but brings to judgment all who would usurp divine sovereignty. God brings to our homeland finally all who make the faith-trek toward it.

A cautionary note. Certainly a veil separates us from the next world. Exploring heaven isn't an exact science, after all—in part because it involves more than our own earthbound desires. What's at stake here is our *hopes,* which rest on God's power to recreate. Like a child waiting to open a Christmas package, we hear one inner voice say, "Wait, don't peek; let it be a surprise!" while another voice says, "It won't hurt to examine the package in anticipation of its contents." Although we can't peek through the wrappings of God's great gift, there are clues in Scripture and in human experience, as noted earlier, to quicken our excitement. It's okay to jiggle the box a little! Joy lies just beyond the thin curtain of the known. God created us with minds to draw analogies and test intuitions, and with spirits to soar upon the Wind. With reverence, then, let's reach imaginatively through the veil at the mystery of heaven. That the risen Lord calls us his friends emboldens us. That Jesus is "preparing a place for us" (John 14:3) invites reverent inquiry, as does the prayer he taught us.

So, with appropriate reverence, let's speculate about society in heaven. First, it's important to acknowledge that heaven is God's right social order, whether here on earth or in the afterlife. Whether come or coming, whether here or there, heaven fulfills our hopes for the peaceable kingdom. What will the kingdom be like in the afterlife? Well, we can extrapolate from what occurs in this life. Because the term *kingdom* is a bit archaic, let's use *community* instead—the community of God. Jesus talked a lot about this community, about how it's already within and among us.

By covenants or agreements of various sorts, people throughout the world live in community. What distinguishes good community from bad? The smooth functioning of at least the following personal interactions: *family, commerce, culture, governance,* and *religion.* Let's explore the heavenly possibilities for each of these relationships.

Family. Family is so basic to life on earth that we can't avoid questions about its role in the next life, where, Jesus said, we neither marry nor are given in marriage. How can we enjoy family if there's no rhythmic pattern of coupling and birth and death? In our earthly experience, *growth* characterizes family relationships: we move from sexual attraction to biological reproduction to children being born and families formed. Much of what *family* means is linked to this time-driven cycle. A young couple falls in love, drawn to each other by physical attraction: by pheromones, by what the eye beholds, by what the ear hears, by shared smells and tastes, by what touch discovers. The young man and woman marry; they bond together emotionally. From their sexual passion babies are born, whose birth is celebrated by parents, siblings, grandparents, great-grandparents, further kinfolk, and a circle of friends and associates. Despite all the attacks on the family that we face today, and the frequency of divorce, and speculation that reproduction might someday (heaven forbid!) become completely commercialized and mechanized, such bonding will surely continue to sustain the family as earth's basic social unit.

So the question comes, what about families in heaven? This is a tough question. After all, family is not only a basic social unit; it's also blessed by religious covenants. The dilemma of the heavenly family is so weighty that it makes some people see the grounds for bodily resurrection as shaky. Tempted to settle for a less material view of heaven, they speculate that perhaps heaven is just the divine memory of who we've been. But let's consider the dilemma carefully:

Using the analogy of seed and stalk, I reasoned earlier that heaven won't *diminish* but rather will *enhance* the values and experiences we enjoy on earth. In a previous chapter I suggested (by analogical reasoning) that the ecstasy experienced in sexual orgasm is a pale intimation of the glory to be experienced by persons within a heavenly milieu blessed by increased dimensionality and enhanced sensory powers. Likewise, I believe that within new boundaries families may continue a bonding based upon a heightened mutuality that far exceeds the joys of procreation. Ponder a family reunion involving not three or four living generations, but dozens. With that new definition of "extended family," it doesn't seem practical to try for a family picnic in heaven! It may be enough to find one's closest and dearest relatives. The logistics of how a family unit might include multiple spouses—exes and *their* exes—is mind-boggling. Expanded and extended families present complications, to be sure; but within practical limits and heightened powers to love, reunions might be possible and fulfilling.

Let's raise our sights above the pattern of earthly bonding, however, in favor of something greater, of which marriage is a prototype. In a typical wedding ceremony people are reminded that marriage is a type of a larger covenant, that of Christ and the church. My own genealogy has been traced back to some fecund tenth-century European prince. A million other people could wend their way back through corridors of time, via genealogical software, to this same progenitor. Even if he's in heaven, though, meeting this ancient ancestor isn't a high priority for me. I'd much rather meet departed friends and neighbors.

But the question of growth persists. Do we rule out babies being born and nourished? One wonders what could supplant the enjoyment of cuddling a baby. One Muslim tradition says that if people in heaven want a baby they can have one—presumably without all the mess and pain now associated with having and raising children, for a baby (says that tradition) will become a young man in an hour![4] This process of heavenly birthing may not be necessary, however—for either girl or boy babies. Until the earth melts with fervent heat there will be lots of babies dying of disease, and plagues, and as victims of some cruel Herod. People in heaven may even now be nurturing the many babies who have died before maturity. What a delightful task for heavenly grandparents! If time and space operate as realities within the context of an encompassing eternal order, then such babies (and growing children) are available to be loved and nurtured and taught by foster parents.

If, as Christians generally assert, Jesus will return to this earth for a time to lead humanity into a kingdom social order, will cycles of growth occur, but without death? Will our planet earth complete its service as a school for heaven and yield to a greater cosmic experience for people to know themselves and others as children of God? Or will earth be reconstituted as one of many worlds available for human families to enjoy in the resurrected life? In the renewed cosmos will persons be perpetually of one age? The early church fathers believed that in heaven each of us will retain that which is significant for each stage of our lives, that our wholeness will encompass the feelings of infancy, childhood, youth, young adulthood, older adulthood, and the senior years, but without the downward drag of aging, diminished energy, memory loss, pain, sickness, or the pangs of remorse. This sounds good to me!

Commerce. Commerce characterizes the city. It entails making or collecting goods (things and ideas) and distributing them. It facilitates exchange of services aimed at optimizing the skills and wellbeing of all. Principled competition and cooperation in a functional society enhance excellence of service. As C. S. Lewis said, "Heaven is a city, and a Body, because the blessed remain eternally different: a society, because each has something to tell all the others."[5]

If we're to be resurrected as persons living harmoniously in the heavenly city, then God's will involves *actions* as well as *attitudes*. How does heaven model obedient behavior in the exchange of goods and services? To answer this question it may be helpful to look at the basic commodities involved in earthly commerce: food, clothing, and shelter. Will our resurrection bodies require food or an equivalent energy source? Probably, for although greatly enhanced, we will remain creatures of God, not ghostly apparitions. Will we need clothing? It's a beneficial social practice on earth (considering the alternative), and it's certainly practical weatherwise in most regions. In my view clothing would be a nice convention to continue in heaven, whether or not the climate requires it. Clothes are especially fulfilling for people who find artistic expression and satisfaction through designing or wearing them. As for jewelry and other accessories, I would guess that our yearning for beauty might lead to some such enjoyments, although I would hope for a management taboo against cultural practices that mutilate and thus dishonor the body.

As for housing, Jesus' teaching about many rooms indicates that heaven provides an equivalent to an apartment or a house. In heaven life will follow a rhythm of activity and rest, as we concluded earlier. This will keep eternity manageable emotionally and provide people with private space. That rhythm is a good thing on earth; it will be good in heaven as well. And the picture of the new heaven and renewed earth found in the book of Revelation indicates that the terrain of heaven will combine the best of the natural and the artificial, the city and the country.

Our earth is abundantly able to support life with required food, clothing, and shelter, but ignorance and sin combine to produce an economy marred by inequity in distribution and overtaxed resources. With love as the motive and truth as the standard, and with the whole cosmos as our realm, surely ways will be found to support equitable distribution of energy, clothing, and shelter, with room to spare for all the other material things that enrich life. There's creativity and excitement in making things and exchanging goods and services. Even shopping can be fun!

Commercial interactions on earth involve more than food, clothing, and shelter, of course. They also provide information exchange, personal and public services, entertainment, and travel experiences. Transportation in heaven will surely *not* include commuter gridlock and plane crashes. So how will we get about— flying carpets, backpack jets? Probably mechanisms much more sophisticated. If Jesus' resurrected body is a clue, along with accounts of angels appearing to a host of other biblical worthies, I surmise that we will transport ourselves not only across but also through space—and with what by earth standards would seem incredible speed. Anyone who has envied a hawk's ability to soar or a whale's to dive can get enthusiastic about heavenly release from present limitations of mobility. How will the laws of physics be adapted to provide for such mobility? I don't know, but I presume that new creations will lead to discovery of "new" laws, which scientists will harmonize with what's already known; and from these laws, new "manuals of operation" will arise.

What about health services? Although freed from death, heavenly creatures will be neither omnipotent nor omniscient. We will likely have accidents in heaven, especially in exercising our stewardship of the cosmos. God's angels may well have to bear *us* up lest *we* dash ourselves against the rocks. Jesus didn't deny the divine power to be lifted to safety when tempted in the wilderness, but rather considered the evocation of such power during his desert sojourn to be an unprincipled way of gaining the kingdoms of the world, a bad means to a good end (see Matt. 4:1–11).

Currently experiments are ongoing to keep life going forever, with some people now in deep freeze awaiting scientific breakthroughs that will enable their broken or debilitated bodies to be revivified. Others look to cloning to replicate the self. But scientific health-care efforts will succeed only in extending life, not in making it everlasting. At best they're intimations of the divine healing that will occur in heaven and bring us into new and eternal life. At worst they're attempts to gain perfection through purely human efforts.

The vision of John the Revelator signifies healthy bodies in a healthy society:

> Then the angel showed me the river of the water of life, bright as crystal, flowing from the throne of God and of the Lamb through the middle of the street of the city. On either side of the

river is the tree of life with its twelve kinds of fruit, producing its fruit each month; and the leaves of the tree are for the healing of the nations. (Rev. 22:1–2)

Language and currency expedite our exchanges of goods and services. Do you remember the Genesis story about the tower of Babel? It relates how God confused human language and scattered the population about the earth so that sinful people couldn't construct a concentrated and powerful civilization in rebellion against divine purpose. God's action was, in effect, a blockade against human usurpation of divine sovereignty, a rebuff to hubris. In heaven, humanity—cleansed from sin and under divine guidance—will be able to build what that tower symbolized: a civilization bridging earth and heaven, synchronizing human and divine will. It will be an inclusive not a parochial social order, a peaceful not a violent one. Achievement of social goals will be by love and truth, not by hate and deceit.

Does the uniqueness of God's covenant with Abraham suggest some version of Hebrew as the language of heaven? It could be, but I surmise that heightened telepathic powers and changed bodies will allow for a language unlike any present earthly tongue. Each earthly language has special capabilities to capture thought and to depict realities, descriptive and conceptual. Each language enriches the human story. So if heaven is composed of multitudes from every culture, a universal language may well be in order, congenial to heightened capacities for sensing, reasoning, and intuiting.

Body language likewise varies from culture to culture. Interpreting such linguistic signs will be an exciting challenge, chock-full of laughter and camaraderie. Does this hand-wave mean come or not? Do lifted eyebrows mean I'm understood or not? Freed from duplicity and guile, smiles and laughter will surely bridge ethnic and cultural differences. In devotional terms the language of heaven is a "new song." What happened at the first Pentecost following Jesus' resurrection offers a clue: persons baptized by the Holy Spirit experienced an ecstasy so powerful they intuitively understood the language of others. Linguistic and cultural barriers melted under the blazing power of the Holy Spirit—heaven came down, and glory filled their souls! If so in Jerusalem then, how much more later, in heaven?

Language is one instrument of social interaction; currency is another medium of exchange. Although based upon sufficiency rather than scarcity, the economy of heaven may involve some form of currency exchange (even if goods are held in common and each works for the benefit of all). The cosmos is a huge place, and if under divine order human beings exercise stewardship over different parts of it with complementary skills, some accounting system for exchange of goods and services may be in order. Why shouldn't accountants and bookkeepers have a chance to use their skills? We remain creatures with limits to understanding, and some need for boundaries. Alternatively, an earthside analogy may be instructive: retirees often volunteer for tasks for the satisfaction of working together on useful community projects. On the other hand, if angels can get along without a system of currency to do the work of God throughout the cosmos, surely incoming human settlers can also.

The arts. Artistic expression arises from the freedom for creativity made possible by exchanges of goods, information, and services, fostered by governance. And, of course, these creative activities depend upon the material world. Arts and crafts reflect creativity in many different ways. In the West patronage for the arts has come from the empire, the church, and more recently the corporation. Under such patronage sublime music and art have been produced, beautiful architecture created, great literature written and read.

Renaissances, however, have a way of running downhill, from the sublime to the ridiculous to the prurient. You don't have to look far for the ridiculous: reflect, for example, upon the hodge-podge of musical clips used to hype hemorrhoid or constipation relief on television ads during the dinner hour. As for the descent into the prurient, consider this example: using the Internet both as a marketplace and as a video medium, a couple sold tickets for people to watch them have sexual intercourse. When interviewed not long ago on a TV program dealing with pornography, the two seemed impervious to shame, rather congratulating themselves for making ten thousand dollars per month peddling their intimacy to pay-for-view voyeurs. At an even lower level of depravity was a case of international child pornography, discovered in the summer of 2002, in which *parents* were charged by the U.S. Customs Commission for sexually exploiting *their own children*.[6] Sin is why artistry falls from heaven to hell, from paeans of praise to the pandering of pornography.

On earth paradise is always getting trashed. In heaven things will be different. The sinful city of man, symbolized in the book of Revelation as "Babylon," will be supplanted by the holy city of God, the "new Jerusalem." Redemption is already in progress, however, for God's kingdom shines as light into darkness and permeates as leaven to make society palatable. That redemptive process will be completed in heaven. Jacques Ellul considers that although the city wasn't God's original plan, he decided to take over humanity's concept. "God does not reject this world of revolt and death," writes Ellul; "he does not annihilate it in the abyss of fire. Rather he adopts it . . . he takes charge of it . . . transforms it into a city with gates of pearl. . . . God does not shatter men's hopes. Rather he fulfills them there."[7]

Heaven offers freedom from artistic degeneration. Some people find it difficult to envision drama or literature without plots involving villainy, deceit, violence, or adultery. They ask: Where would one find pathos if everyone were good, as presumably they will be in heaven? Won't a heavenly equivalent of politically correct literature be predictable and boring? The answer is no: artistic creativity doesn't require sin to make its genres effective. Fears about erosion of aesthetic creation are understandable, though, for it's hard to peer beyond the horizon of our experience. Yet such fears reflect an inadequate vision of the resurrected life. To experience the uplifting of spirit is the most thrilling of life's experiences. Consider comedy that makes you laugh, but not at the expense of another. Reflect upon poetry that brings tears to your eyes, paintings that put you in rapture, music that gives you goosebumps, courageous rescues of sailors at sea or miners underground that thrill you, love experiences that lift you to heights of passion, human and divine. These good things of civilization won't be lost in heaven. Nor will the best moments of all on earth—those moments in your life when faith surges and you feel yourself transported into the very presence of the Most High! Do you lack words adequate to describe such moments of ecstasy? Look inside! For a few moments, at least, you've been in heavenly places. Expect eternal life to be enriched like that, but beyond what we can now measure, and rejoice that such richness will be enduring.

In heaven, as on earth, effective drama portrays good triumphing over evil. I daresay the vastness and the openness of the restored universe will offer adventures adequate for epic tales, just as it will provide raw material for the visual arts, for painting, for sculpture, for architecture. The book of Revelation envisions the future kingdom in terms of splendor—gates of pearl, streets of gold, every kind of tree. In each glorious sunset God signifies a creation filled with beauty. Every violin sonata reminds us that the whole universe vibrates with divine reality.

Governance. Government aims to ensure fair distribution of goods and services and to provide opportunities for people to express themselves creatively and to live as neighbors who respect each other. Good government fosters community by providing freedom, economic security, safe circumstances, and education. Under oppressive circumstances artists have used their gifts to defy tyranny, and have frequently suffered for doing so. John the Revelator did this with his poetry. In captivity he stood up to tyrant Rome, and his metaphors about a heavenly city changed the tide of history. In an apocalyptic drama this banned poet cryptically pictured an ungodly "Babylon" at world's end summoned to divine judgment by a trumpet-blowing angel and a heavenly choir that proclaimed triumphantly: "The kingdom of the world has become the kingdom of our Lord and of his Messiah, and he will reign forever and ever" (Rev. 11:15). It's the victory of the Lamb!

In the twentieth century a Russian poet, Boris Pasternak, announced judgment upon ungodly governance to good effect. Throughout history poets similarly have served prophetic roles. These poets focus God's wrath upon evil. They awaken consciences. They force us to lift our eyes above covetousness. They spell injustice in stanzas dripping with blood. They nag us out of indifference. Directly or indirectly, they witness to that Eternal City whose architect and builder is God, and by their rhetoric they stir us toward its holiness. We need such artistry, for without godly governance anarchy reigns, chaos destroys commerce, creativity wanes, plagues run rampant, and people lack time and energy to make human community function.

If on earth we're to emulate heaven, what characterizes the politics of heaven? Who will govern in the peaceable kingdom? Jesus will. And we will participate according to our gifts. An old architectural axiom says that form follows function. Let's apply this axiom to governance, to consider how delegated authority in a realm without sin might function. The government resting on the Messiah's shoulders will certainly differ from what humanity has experienced in its long history. In the first place, the peaceable kingdom requires no armies, moats, land mines, or fortifications (including Strategic Defense Initiative). No stealth bombers, spy networks, bombs (dumb or smart) are needed. Heaven will be filled with people from every nook and cranny of the world, from every ethnic group; but there will be no slave ships, no intertribal slaughter over control of oil or diamonds or prestige. No hacking off children's hands, no slaughtering daughters who convert to another religion, no ethnic purging, no religious wars, no costly penal system.

On earth military defense is a major aspect of governance. (In fact, some extremists think that that's the *only* proper governmental role.) If, in some future aeon, inhabitants of hell rebel again against heaven, I expect the angels to handle the threat. We're told in Scripture that hell is for the devil and his ilk. "A great chasm has been fixed" in heaven against it (Luke 16:26). Under God those who govern on earth and in heaven are to increase the good, not just restrain the evil. The wrath of God is our protection against evil, and the love of God is our support for good.

So what kind of governmental infrastructure may be needed in heaven? A greatly reduced one; that's for sure. Try tabulating what evil costs *your* community to get a feeling for sin's terrible cost in human time and money to earthly governments. Nonetheless, some judiciary function would seem appropriate for heaven. In numerous passages the Bible speaks of Judgment "Day." We tend to picture this as a single event with Jesus on the throne routing people to hell or to heaven. Given the nature of time within eternity, however, it may be more appropriate to consider the great Judgment Day as an ongoing event after every person's death, at least until the end of time on earth. In any case, heaven will surely vindicate before the bar of God all oppressed persons, the "disappeared ones," the wrongly imprisoned, victims of holocausts and scam artists, babies tossed into garbage bins, aboriginal people slaughtered by conquerors, rivals killed by jealous rulers, persons raped or sold into sex slavery. Heaven will make victims whole in ways that honor their dignity as persons created in the divine image.

In the year 2001 a news special featured a Christian agency that gathered in the "lost boys" of Sudan, children who had trekked across African countries, risking death by starvation, disease, murder, and rapacious lions. They had fled tribal wars that destroyed their families. Some of these boys had eventually found new homes in North Dakota, and although the weather was cold beyond what they had experienced, the warmth of love and acceptance more than made up for climatic and cultural dislocation. These sojourners found "the bosom of Abraham." Such children join a myriad of other sufferers who by faith looked for a city with foundations. They're part of God's pilgrim band, along with heroes of faith in other centuries. Heaven's judiciary will surely offer redemptive justice to all persons who have suffered from human sin.

Heaven's judicial system may extend minimally to adjudicate honest differences. I say *minimally*, because heaven certainly won't allow cutthroat and litigious competition. There will be room for everyone, an abundance of goodwill. We will remain creatures with limits, though, and may differ in judgments that require submission to judicial review. (Even angels may disagree, for all we know!) This aspect of the heavenly judiciary will be like having an umpire for baseball games.

Given the complexity of the cosmos, a bureau of standards might be an appropriate function of governance. *(We're really speculating now! Remember my cautionary note earlier in this chapter?)* A uniform taxonomy of weights, measurements, technological components, communication signals, and transportation rules could be useful to enhance creativity and increase the common good in a cosmos with billions of people living and interacting together. (Voilà—the metric system, at last!) Some sort of registry to keep track of people and their skills would seem helpful as well. Energy, education, communication, transportation, commerce, and the arts categorize major functions of the human community, earthside as in heaven; and godly governance in all these arenas—whether on earth or in heaven—frees people to act creatively and for the common good.

By God's design government is to be a servant, not a master. Sin spoils this design whenever the ego tries to usurp divine prerogatives. Then power corrupts and governance fails or is badly diminished. Political history is a long recital of that failure to follow God's will on earth. There are bright chapters in that history, however, for which we praise God, times when people understand themselves in covenant with God. Government *does* work among people of goodwill on earth. We have seen it, participated in it, been blessed by it. We anticipate government in heaven to serve humanity fully. What we've glimpsed in the humble service of godly men and women earthside offers a foretaste of the kind of governance to expect in heaven. Perhaps the political motto should be amended to read: government of the people, by the people, for the people, under the rule of a sovereign God. In heaven God's covenant with humanity will find fulfillment. We will serve according to our giftedness.

Scientists, teachers, artisans, farmers, merchants, and artists require a social structure to find personal fulfillment and to contribute value to others. The word *commonwealth* conveys this idea. Heaven will be a wealth of people from every cultural and linguistic group, with diverse traditions and customs. With a cosmos freed from sin and with inhabitants guided by the twin goals of truth and love, human beings can become fully co-creators with God.

A political structure adequate for the commonwealth of heaven may require local and regional officials to make decisions about energy distribution and recycling, development projects, educational, artistic, and communication facilities and staffing, intergalactic exploration, and scientific investigation. Local governance may be *ad hoc* or ongoing; it may be like New England town meetings, with everyone involved, or strictly representative. Whatever form it takes, though, governance will certainly come easier among people whose resurrection bodies preclude sinful motivations. Imagine a world freed from sin's terrible personal and social burden, where minds and hearts are in tune with God, ready to explore the terrain of heaven with joy, and eager to serve the cosmos as excited stewards. This is indeed good news! With fear and trembling, reluctant to leave existence as we know it, we will cross the deep abyss of death confident in reaching humanity's true community, the ultimate promised land.

Religion. Religion leavens the whole of society with respect for truth, for God, and for others. It offers light in which to see the world about us from a divine perspective. The fear of the Lord is the foundation of knowledge. All truth is ultimately revealed. Curiously, religion as it's practiced on earth may have a limited function in heaven. On earth, religion is a witness to the kingdom of God. Its prophets through the ages have proclaimed God's will and exposed personal and social evils. Its preachers have spread the good news of salvation to the sinful and the ignorant. Its evangelists have reaped the harvest of the Holy Spirit. Its congregations have lifted up the oppressed, gathered in the outcast, healed the sick, and restored the broken. Its pastors have consoled the bereaved and eased their pain. Its teachers have educated the ignorant. Its congregations have lifted heavenward concerts of prayer on behalf of righteousness and truth. Its members have demonstrated the compassion of Jesus in myriad ways. In short, religious organizations have served as embassies of the heavenly city.

In the society of the glorified, worship may achieve a balance between spontaneity and order only approximated earthside. Heaven won't require as much organization, for we will be taught directly by our Lord. As seventeenth-century theologian Richard Baxter observed, prayer and preaching become obsolete when their goals have been attained.[8] John the Revelator envisioned no temple in the new Jerusalem, for the Lord God Almighty and the Lamb constitute the temple (21:22). The apostle Paul insisted that our bodies are the temples of the Holy Spirit. This is where God dwells—within us, among us. Tents, tabernacles, cathedrals, chapels, sanctuaries, meetinghouses—these presently serve as places of worship. They constitute dedicated property, holy ground. In heaven they will no longer be needed. No more fussing over turf, material or ecclesiastical. For in heaven human bodies and human communities will be wholly in sync with the sovereign Lord. They will be attuned fully to a renewed social order. Thus they will join with all the rest of creation to proclaim in word and deed throughout the cosmos, "Glory, glory, glory!"

NINE

The Renewed Cosmos

The material universe is both an essential display of the greatness and goodness of God and the arena of the eternal life of finite spirits, including the human.[1]
—*Dallas Willard*

As our generation marvels at our new view of the universe—our way of asserting the world's coherence— we are fulfilling our part, contributing our rung to the human ladder reaching for the stars.[2]
—*Brian Greene*

There will be new planets to develop, new principles to discover, new joys to experience. Every moment of eternity will be an adventure of discovery.[3]
—*Ray C. Stedman*

For the creation waits with eager longing for the revealing of the children of God; for the creation was subjected to futility, not of its own will but by the will of the one who subjected it, in hope that the creation itself

will be set free from its bondage to decay and will obtain
the freedom of the glory of the children of God.[4]

—*Paul of Tarsus*

W hat does it mean for the cosmos to be renewed? To answer
that question, let's first ponder the intriguing mystery of
the universe, then consider secular forecasts (both pessimistic and
optimistic) for a cosmic future, and finally reflect upon the dreams
of God's covenant people.

THE MYSTERY OF THE UNIVERSE

With increasing sophistication and with greater technological
tools, cosmologists now probe deep into the past, seeking to map
the explosion of the cosmos from its beginning, estimated at twelve
to fifteen billion years ago, and constructing computer models to
account for and depict the flow of mass and energy through time
and space. One thing is clear from their studies: the cosmos is
much larger, much more complex, and in much greater flux than
earlier imagined. Many of these scientists are God-fearing people
who envision the universe still being flung from the hand of the
Almighty! They find their faith and their science fused at the cusp
of cosmic mystery, and it fills them with wonder. From reading
what these physicists, biologists, and cosmologists write, I find my
mind buzzing with questions. My curiosity hasn't dampened my
faith or lessened my contentment with the mystery of resurrection
hope. I wonder, though, how people in heaven will experience the
cosmos.

Some scientists believe that there may be ten or possibly eleven
dimensions of reality. As noted earlier, we're reasonably at home in
three of them now—length, width, and depth—four if we include

time. According to these scientists other dimensions are "curled up" (another scientific metaphor!), meaning that they elude direct detection.[5] Will multiple dimensions require radically new or adapted bodies? Will there be gravitational fields and chemical components regulated by independent variables of local planetary time to provide different boundaries for creaturely activities? Will the renewed cosmos be a steady-state universe, or a continuously expanding one?

I expect you've asked yourself such questions (or similar ones), too. Let's examine some forecasts about the cosmic future.

SECULAR FORECASTS

Pessimistic secular forecasts for the future of the cosmos. Some secular forecasts of the world's future are downright gloomy, especially as envisioned by social scientists. They see our technological world poised on the edge of disaster of a magnitude never before experienced by humanity. The disease AIDS, now pandemic in Africa, provides an omen for what might occur if and when the lower orders of nature unleash their fury upon the higher orders. So consider the following possible doomsday scenarios, some potentially intermingled:

The nuclear power hidden in submarines and mountain silos gets out of hand by error or by demonic madness, and civilization is devastated for millennia. Plagues, barely contained hitherto, are unleashed and spread within global society. Microorganisms replace horses and tanks and stealth bombers as weapons in wars that defeat the conquered and the conquerors alike, wars that destroy not just forest villages but mega-cities as populous as São Paulo, Mexico City, Shanghai, and New York. The rich countries and corporations so plunder the forests of poor countries to keep their own woods pristine for affluent hikers that the resultant global warming leads to global desertification and subsequent large-scale starvation. Energy wars get out of hand and destroy the technological society they were purported to save. Terrorism increases in sophistication and magnitude, putting the people of the world into a state of paralyzing fear that makes eighteenth-century piracy resemble comic opera. A nuclear accident propels humanity into another dark age, and the admired artifacts of the twenty-first century—the skyscrapers, the sports stadiums, the freeways, the Disney Worlds—become like the pyramids of Giza or the clay soldiers of Xian: something to be unearthed and admired millennia later. A different kind of doomsday possibility: an asteroid hits Europe, the Middle East, or America and destroys most of animal life on the planet, including humanity. Our sun burns out and all life in the solar system dies.

All of these grim forecasts for the future seem distressingly possible. Will one of them be realized? Who knows?

Optimistic secular forecasts for the future of the cosmos. Fortunately, there are less gloomy predictions, too. In one of the epigraphs at the head of this chapter, Brian Greene used the phrase "reaching for the stars" to describe expectations of scientists about a cosmic future. Reasoned expectations of these futurists are often nurtured by the fantasies of more intuitive dreamers: science fiction writers. In their way, these writers probe eternity. Their genre involves imagining events across enormous stretches of time. Science fiction writers often picture humanity spreading across the cosmos and using techniques of genetic and electronic engineering to extend individual life not hundreds, but thousands of years. These secular futurists conjure up brain-implanted information disks that impart almost instant knowledge—no laborious study required. They envision a universe increasingly under human control through enhanced technology, although not without intergalactic wars and threats by microcosmic forces seeking to thwart human evolution.

Using exotic yet-to-be-harnessed forces, modified human beings in science fiction stories travel at speeds measured by parsecs and light-years.

Space enthusiasts in the science fiction genre are abandoning chemical propellants in favor of harnessing solar energy, as on space stations currently. They envision using tethers like slingshots to hurl us from planet to planet. They conjure up modes for traveling highways of light rather than highways of concrete. Robots and biotech organisms (both of which serve their human masters) are featured in these authors' modern tales. Arthur Clarke's *3001* has dinosaurs so genetically domesticated that they do the gardening chores and even serve as babysitters![6] And if worse comes to worst and the sun burns out in a few billion years, before alternate places are found for biological life, some sci-fi futurists envision the human race living forever through electronic clones that adapt to otherwise hostile environments and keep intelligence flowing throughout an expanding cosmos—until it, too, burns to ashes in a silent death.[7]

David Brin, in his stories, imaginatively posits a variety of creatures evolving from pre-sentience to sentience, with fits and starts over millions of years under the tutelage of higher-level patrons—an upward path, in other words. He posits, for example, that high-sentient-level cosmic management will require some planets to lie fallow for millions of years. In one line a protagonist says, "If the universe seems to be trying to destroy you, the best way to fight is with hope." Over long stretches of time and across intergalactic space, Brin quests for a cosmic, evolutionary purpose greater than personal goals of wealth and power, greater than corporate goals of race or clan or gods, "a purpose higher than all those things." The hope of sentient creatures, he writes, is "never to let go the capacity to dream. To weave the illusions that help us all make it through the dark, dark night."[8]

Not just scientists, but ordinary people are also optimistic about the future of the world as we know it. It must be acknowledged that over the past century the dreams of futurists have led to important discoveries and experiments by more scientific thinkers, resulting, for example, in medical advances undreamed of a few decades ago. Medical engineering and pharmacological science offer hope for a good life to persons suffering from a variety of debilitating and crippling diseases. So do minimally invasive surgery and new drugs for blocking disease. In technologically advanced countries, life is being extended. Optimists hope for 120 years as a normal life expectancy for healthy persons during the *current* century. Death is being pushed back, at least for fortunate folks in stable societies. (The poor in urban slums are typically—unfortunately—excluded from the benefits of technological advances.) So consider, if you will, these optimistic scenarios:

Recent and anticipated discoveries and inventions bring an extended era of peace and health to humanity—a new golden age—with people living actively for centuries. Carbon tubes permit the construction of elevators into space, and per-fluorocarbon technology enables engineers to warm Mars (recently discovered to have water) and make it habitable, thus relieving earth's overcrowding. Gene therapy curtails violent predispositions and fosters cooperative societies. Global religious awakenings occur among people sufficiently horrified at the bloody violence of the twentieth century to humble themselves before the Almighty; as a consequence of such penitence, increased numbers of medical teams do reconstructive surgery for victims of land mines around the world and inoculate all children against diseases. Pharmaceutical companies gladly donate drugs to curb infectious diseases in less technically developed countries. Corporations serve all their clients equitably. Global agreements even out the distribution of goods and services. Wealthy nations help poor ones achieve economic stability, fulfilling the ancient prophecy of turning swords into plowshares. The burden of third-world debt is lifted. Every year is a Jubilee. Habitat for Humanity models compassionate community assistance worldwide. Justice prevails in the courts. Marriage covenants endure. Peace blesses the Middle East, Africa, and Ireland. Military expenditures are reduced and education funds increased. Religious leaders depend upon the power of truth rather than upon coercion or violence to advance their causes. The kingdom of God becomes a guiding concept for all humanity.

Renewals in righteousness have occurred periodically in the past among penitent people captivated by God's Spirit. Could they happen again? Yes. On a global scale? It's *possible,* in the providence of God. But is it probable?

Such optimistic social and political forecasts generally feature an idealism that seems impractically utopian to war-weary contemporary people. These dreams of a progressively improving earthly future for humanity are founded on an unstated hope that humankind has been crafted in the image of the Divine and is destined for better things than continued violence, injustice, and deceit; and the belief that the universe is somehow able to, and ought to, sustain that vision of the good life. The implementation of these optimistic dreams would require cooperation and rationality at a level not yet widely experienced by humanity.

In the implementation of *their* hopes and dreams, sci-fi scenarios are generally more realistic. They typically feature brain and brawn, not spirit, in the struggle between good and evil. Intrigue and violence mark the plots, with little or no reverence before the Lord Almighty, maker of heaven and earth. The odysseys of the future elite space-warriors of fiction are as conflict-ridden as their prototypes in the Greek pantheon. These sci-fi stories tend to replay Babylon the Fallen, not Jerusalem the Golden. They neither dramatize nor envision Isaiah's peaceable kingdom. Like an intergalactic cloud, hubris swirls around the literature of these space dreamers, as it does around more prosaic humanistic social dreamers. *Seeds of truth have been planted, nonetheless; and in God's good timing, with God's direction, these seeds will grow.*

Yes, oh yes, the human yearning for an eternal homeland lurks silently in the shadows of these stories. The eternal Word can be heard in the heartbeat of hope within such sagas of the future. God's Word can be discerned within the organizational charts of political planners. This Word can be discerned in the jargon of working scientists who for a quarter of a century have been steering and tracking Voyagers I and II on treks past Jupiter, Saturn, Uranus, and Neptune—and will continue tracking them until these mechanical extensions of our senses exit the solar system for an isolated destiny in space, carrying earth's greetings to the universe, some forty thousand years into the future.

For all these dreams of future human glory on this earth, *death is still the last enemy;* and sooner or later it confronts every person and must be faced. In both science fiction and scientific research one discerns earnest, creative minds groping for an angelic hand to lead humanity back through Eden's flaming sword, freed from pain, no longer trapped in a thicket of thorns, rescued from sinful fratricide and its awful holocausts, into the very paradise of God. Even without attribution these secular dreamers are not to be faulted for reading the book of God's created order more creatively than most people, or for lifting from that book the laws of an order that lets us live more wholesomely on the earth. In the omnipotence of God, they too are agents of human hope.

DREAMS OF GOD'S COVENANT PEOPLE

In the phrase used by Dallas Willard at the heading of this chapter, Christians envision the cosmos as the arena of eternal life.

Believers find inadequate all approaches to cosmic renewal that exclude God from human salvation, although they acknowledge that God works redemptively within all human systems of thought and action. Believers focus instead upon spirit as the reality supportive of mind and body in bringing health and wholeness to the person, to society, and to the cosmos. Accordingly, they ask, What are *God's* plans for human wholeness? How can technologies present and future fit into the final assault upon life's last enemy? How can entropy be overcome without as well as within, in the cosmos as well as in the individual? What does it take to cope with the destroyer, sin? How can death be overcome?

Let's look now at some religious perspectives on the future of the cosmos as the arena for life eternal. These perspectives encompass both pessimism and optimism. Given how our civilization tacks between good and evil, the human ability to reassemble stuff and energy into new forms is both a bane and a blessing. For centuries rearranging stuff was a fairly harmless tinkering with materials—converting clay to bricks, sand to glass, oil to energy, wolves to dogs, ore to metal, catgut to violin strings, logs to lumber and newsprint, soils to agriculture, and so on. In recent decades, tinkering with molecules and nuclei has upped the ante. Our now-global civilization, though incredibly wealthy and inventive, nonetheless totters on the edge of disaster; indeed, disaster looms incrementally more ominously with each passing year.

Consider some areas of tension between good and evil. Organ "farms" provide genetically altered pig tissue for use in repairing the human body. The stem-cell transplant technique has been mastered, and controversy rages over use of surplus human eggs fertilized *in vitro*. Corporations vie for control of incredibly volatile and valuable genetic data and procedures. These developments may aid health and for the favored few may extend life, but they may also create generational strife and social chaos. Software rules the information age and ratchets up the conflict. Technical advances project a future that exhibits a merging of artificial and human intelligence, with memory chips implanted in the brain, with nanomachines (ten times smaller than a human hair) clearing debris from aging arteries every evening. Despite strong moral reservations, the cloning of human beings looms on the near horizon and will probably occur. Will it be a tool for good or for ill?

Theists project an end of the cosmos as we know it—and not necessarily aeons from now. Call them pessimists, if you will, but *realists* may be a better term. They believe that the end of present earthly existence will occur after humanity aspires—as did ancient counterparts, but with exponentially greater power—to build a tower to heaven (literally or figuratively), contrary to God's blueprints. As technology advances, the stakes keep getting larger in the cosmic contest of good and evil. Knowing the terrible power of evil, but also—and with gladness of heart—the triumphant power of the risen Lord to redeem, believers find it credible to anticipate that in an apocalyptic conflagration sometime (next year, next century, next millennium, the far-distant future) and by some means God will destroy evil and reconstruct the cosmos. In the imagery of John the Revelator, Satan—the deceiver, the destroyer—will be cast into the lake of fire (Rev. 21:8). Thus God will close the chapter of earthly history in the book of life and bring the whole cosmos into heavenly joy and splendor, to the choral applause of myriads of angels and saints gathered around the throne-room of heaven to witness the final scene in the drama of redemption: the material universe transformed. This is optimistic dreaming at its best!

Envisioning the renewed cosmos. What will the cosmos as an arena for eternal life look like? Before tools of modern science revealed the complex nature of matter, some religious thinkers characterized "hard" stuff as sin-laden reality, and "soft" stuff as goodness-laden reality. Accordingly, they depicted God's redemptive enterprise moving toward the ethereal, the vaporous, the intangible. That was how they saw death conquered. For them the holy was really "hole-y." Artistic imagination portrayed angels as wispy creatures, not quite real—soft, not hard. These early thinkers did, however, intuit in light a basic metaphor for spiritual reality. They believed that heavenly restoration reduced substantive, external reality. To strengthen the concept of inner reality, terms such as *transparent* and *crystalline* were appropriated. Divine judgment was seen as fire (a form of light), which separated evil from good by destroying materiality. In short, heaven's mystery was reduced from hard to hazy reality, from stuff to auras. This reduction was the medieval way of showing that a heavenly body is of greater reality than an earthly one.

Picturing heavenly existence as shadowy compared to earthly existence misses the crux of resurrection hope, however—a hope that offers something *more* substantial than what we experience in this life. A laughing baby is "softer" than a "hard" rock, but a higher form of reality. Super-nature, not sub-nature defines the shape of our hope. Re-creation is no more difficult for God than is creation. Both lie within divine power. The book of Revelation uses the most precious substances known to ordinary experience—gold and rubies and pearls—to depict the splendor of the heavenly city.

Believers see human redemption as a key to recreating the universe. Redemption is the trigger mechanism for renewal, at least as far as human beings are concerned. The apostle Paul described the universe as "groaning" under the burden of sin, awaiting the redemption and resurrection of human beings (Rom. 8:23). Noted European theologian Oscar Cullman writes that deliverance of the cosmos from its bondage to sin "will come when the power of the Holy Spirit transforms all matter."[9] How a reconstructed cosmos will be reconfigured can only be hinted at. The cosmos available to our instructed senses appears to have been exploding "outward" from the beginning—whatever that signifies. Cosmic debris gets scattered onto and collected by stars and planets. Burned-out stars collapse and are sucked into the whirling vortices of black holes. Might black holes be God's recycling centers for the creation of new worlds? I would hope that cosmologists and physicists, prayerfully seeking wisdom from God, might focus less upon projecting how the cosmos may die and more upon its possible reconfigurations, and upon how human beings might relate to such a cosmic Eden.

The renewal of the cosmos will be morally significant, because it will entail purgation of sin and evil. Freed from the burden of sin, and with a resurrection body equipped to work within new dimensions, humanity will be able to access much more of the cosmos, and with greater clarity of purpose. The wonders of the present universe won't be diminished; they will be made more congenial to life, offering opportunity for enriched experiences. The future of the cosmos lies not in slime mold, but in higher forms of flora and fauna.

The renewed cosmos of eternity will not be such a lonely place as today's vast, uncharted world. Unfettered by present limitations, we'll be able to satisfy our curiosity about what lies beyond the realms of our present knowledge. Personally, I would like to explore the moons of our solar system—to enjoy the ice volcanoes of Neptune's moon Titon, or the gigantic lava flows of Jupiter's moon Io. I'm thrilled to be a part of the cosmos as it is (what a beautiful planet earth is!) and excited about the prospect of space adventures. I'm more thrilled, however, to anticipate a universe no longer hostile, but swarming with life enveloped in the holiness of God!

Biblical doctrine teaches that God created humanity for the sake of companionship. What a beautiful thought: God creates each new person with special mental, physical, and spiritual endowments so that heaven won't be lonely! How incredible to learn that God not only loves me but needs me and wants me around! And that he needs and wants my neighbors, known and unknown to me, as well as the cosmos, with all its things and its creatures great and small. The *imago Dei* is the basis for God's gift of eternal life to us.

This divine stamp within us results in a certain tension between the natural and the artificial, between wilderness and city. As human beings we stand both within and outside of the rest of nature. It's because we have a special ability to rearrange things that some fervent ecologists consider their own species to be spoilers of nature, some even opining that the universe would be better off without *Homo sapiens*. Stupidity and cupidity in regard to our stewardship give some bite to this charge, but not to their gloomy analysis. I don't think that porpoises or bears or raptors or reptiles or frogs or cows or dogs or trees or grass or mosquitoes or bacteria or viruses ever asked these super-zealots to speak on their behalf. Nor did God. God may, however, use these surly doomsayers to chide the rest of us for careless stewardship—for the sins of greed and lust and pride—and prod us into a more responsible sharing of, and caring for, the creation.

The covenant dream includes overcoming earthly distortions. I see heaven as a blending of the natural and artificial according to a divine blueprint. Gone will be the coarse brutality of primitive aeons. Gone the grinding poverty of failing subsistence systems. Gone the sophisticated brutality of technological society. Present will be the glories of the primitive, the great forests, the pure streams, the stillness of an Arctic night, the sonorous cadence of crickets on a summer evening, the beauty of sunsets over the prairie. Present the structures of the city, more beautiful and functional than medieval cathedrals or modern corporate towers or sports stadiums. Heaven is depicted biblically as the city of God, with verdant, healing trees lining streets of the city with transparent beauty.

God has covenanted with humanity for the care of this earth. This covenant of stewardship remains in force today, even though sin has diminished its effectiveness. In a relatively short time human intelligence has transformed planet earth. In spite of terrible misapplication of God's principles, these creatures made in the divine image have brought about marvelous discoveries and inventions. Human intelligence has harnessed energies for creative enterprises that bring health to the body, delight to the mind, and joy to the spirit. Human stewards of the earth now probe inner and outer space. Their restlessness evidences a God-implanted curiosity and a yearning to be co-creators with the Divine. Purified in heaven from the curse of sin (and adapted physically to multiple planetary systems), creative humanity will join the Master Architect in cosmic reconstruction.

What the cosmos restored in righteousness will look like materially, and how it will incorporate our earth, our solar system, our galaxy (and the billions of others we know of and hypothesize), and human artifacts, we cannot say. We *can* infer that through creative application it will embody the classic longings of the heart: the good, the true, and the beautiful; and that humanity will share in shaping God's own dreams—dreams for the peaceable kingdom.

Understanding time in the context of the covenant dream. Time itself will surely change—at least as humanly experienced. As noted earlier, resurrected life signifies both extension (everlastingness) and "intension" (eternalness).

The term "arrow of time" describes reciprocal events among created objects within the physical universe. Stars and galaxies feed on each other, ocean and landmasses contend, organisms interact symbiotically, ionic exchanges occur, light triumphs over darkness. At a more mundane level, termites and rust destroy our houses, and gasoline keeps our cars going. From its dramatic moment of birth the whole cosmos depicts a rhythmic dance of mass and energy. Ours is not a static universe, but a changing one. In many ways its structure shows disequilibrium. Construing time as a measurement of energy-flow grounds our inquiry into purpose. What explains forward direction? Why do we look back upon what is past and ahead to what is future?

One response suggests that time bends backward upon itself in endless cosmic cycles of death/rebirth, expansion/regression. Such a cyclical view fosters fatalism in human society. Another response suggests that human beings simply impose purpose upon a purposeless universe, consonant with their own and observed experiences of organisms moving from birth to death. For theists, however, the arrow of time signifies a purposive, God-directed, cosmic, continuing extension of intelligence and consciousness in an open and changing cosmos. Biochemist Arthur Peacocke posits a view that "God gives existence to each instant of physical time . . . fecund with possibilities not yet actualized."[10]

In heaven, clock/calendar time won't be for us an earthbound horizontal line from birth to death, but rather a multifaceted measuring of changes, like arrows radiating to circumference, in a cosmos forever expanding. For persons in heaven as on earth, "lived time" marks a cognitive response of living creatures to sequences occurring within a purposive world, involving the interaction of energy, material substance, and spirit. Here again, we sense a tension between continuity and discontinuity. Although we reach out for it, time eludes our grasp. It hovers always on the edge of our understanding. The horizon of observed reality recedes continuously, wrapped in a mystery so elusive and compelling it invites awed exploration.

That we instinctively seek to understand time itself testifies to the voice of God within, to that yen for eternity planted in the heart. "Deep calling to deep" is how an ancient pastoral poet expressed his longing for God's presence in uncertain circumstances (Ps. 42:7). The mystery of time within eternity will be revealed more clearly when sin and death are gone.

For now, though, we can experiment with looking at time in ways other than as linear progression. We can consider ongoing life as musical cadence, for example. We can feel its intricate and passionate rhythms, its range of expression, from piercing tones to throbbing beat almost below audible level, blending with tactile perception. Jürgen Moltmann aptly says that cosmic renewal is "like a great song or a splendid poem or a wonderful dance" showing God's fullness. "The laughter of the universe is God's delight. It is the universal Easter laughter."[11] The words of the apostle Peter express our hope in what is to come in space/time, where "righteousness is at home." These words recharge our faith to witness the presence of heaven on earth and to anticipate with excitement the great day of cosmic reconfiguration:

> But the day of the Lord will come like a thief, and then the heavens will pass away with a loud noise, and the elements will be dissolved with fire, and the earth and everything that is done on it will be disclosed. Since all these things are to be dissolved in this way, what sort of persons ought you to be in leading lives of holiness and godliness, waiting for and hastening the coming of the day of God, because of which the heavens will be set ablaze and dissolved, and the elements will melt with fire? But, in accordance with his promise, we wait for new heavens and a new earth, where righteousness is at home. Therefore, beloved, while you are waiting for these things, strive to be found by him at peace, without spot or blemish. (2 Pet. 3:10–14)

CONCLUSION

Believing, hoping and loving
with my *whole heart,* with my *whole mind*
and with my *whole strength,*
may I be carried to you, beloved Jesus,
as to the goal of all things . . .
the redeemer of the lost,
the savior of the redeemed,
the hope of exiles,
the strength of laborers,
the sweet solace of anguished spirits,
the crown and imperial dignity of the triumphant,
the unique reward and joy
of all the citizens of heaven.[1]
—*St. Bonaventure*

See the universe growing luminous like the horizon
just before sunrise.[2]
—*Teilhard de Chardin*

I give them eternal life, and they will never perish.
No one will snatch them out of my hand.[3]
—*Jesus*

The hope of heaven is a beacon guiding us on our earthly journey. We see a Light ahead, beyond the vale of death; and we follow that Light, although what it beckons us to find at the horizon of earthly time remains a mystery. Intimations of heaven are imprinted in our minds and engraved upon our culture. These personal and corporate dreams and visions mold the psyche and offer opportunities to seek and find the good, the true, and the beautiful. Our hopes for an afterlife are expressed in stories etched on cave walls and enshrined in art and literature. The resurrection of Jesus Christ assures us that such ancient and enduring visions, even if crudely articulated, derive from our Creator and Redeemer. With fear and trembling we have dared pull out and look at the maps of heaven. With maps in hand we have peered across the great divide to check heaven's terrain, to learn about its inhabitants, to ponder our place there socially and individually in a renewed cosmos whose dimensions and opportunities for creative participation with the Creator stagger the mind. Yes, they stagger the mind, but they exhilarate the spirit!

A concluding prudent word is appropriate, however. To use an old sales adage, "The map is not the territory." If our hopes for heaven were too lucid, we would shirk our responsibility on earth, neglecting to learn how to live as persons created in God's image. If our hopes were too opaque, we would despair, crushed by tragedy and beaten in a losing duel with death. In either case, we would fail to live faithfully in God's kingdom. *It is in our earthly home that we must freely respond to the divine initiative. It is here and now that we must let God overcome the sin in our lives and in our communities. It is on earth that God redeems and sanctifies us in preparation to live in eternity according to the divine image stamped on our hearts.*

So, then, earth is a province of heaven, albeit a sin-laden one. It's one where God suffers with us and patiently teaches us what's true and righteous. Here on earth God redeems us from sin's curse and snatches us from Satan, the destroyer. Thus humbled, forgiven, schooled in holiness, we anticipate with gladness the gift of eternal life in a new creation, finally and fully formed in righteousness. Yes, we accept God's gracious gift. We welcome God's promise to dry our tears, to forgive our sins, to heal our infirmities, to defeat evil and death, to bring justice, and to gather the world's people into true unity with each other, and into engagement with all the energy, mind, and matter in the universe. Isaiah's imagery of the holy mountain of Jerusalem provides a prophetic forecast of what God offers all humanity:

And he will destroy on this mountain the shroud that is cast over all peoples, the sheet that is spread over all nations; he will swallow up death forever. Then the Lord GOD will wipe away the tears from all faces, and the disgrace of his people he will take away from all the earth, for the LORD has spoken. It will be said on that day, Lo, this is our God; we have waited for him, so that he might save us. This is the LORD for whom we have waited; let us be glad and rejoice in his salvation. (Isa. 25:7–9)

Lord, on that great day may we, along with Job, hear the morning stars sing together and all the heavenly beings shout for joy! Praise your holy name!

As Carol Zaleski notes, "What Christians hope for is not a pleasant dream but a complete awakening, compared to which our present existence will look like troubled sleep."[4]

EPILOGUE

YOU WILL LIVE ON

My friend, we mourn your death
but cherish your immortality.
You will live on.
You will live on in progeny
shaped by your example
of integrity and concern.
You will live on in memories
recalled in stories told
our children's children.
You will live on as a page
in the book of life, cherished
forever by the Creator.
You will live on when memory
fades into oblivion,
when our sun burns out.
You will live on in a body
resurrected, like that of Jesus,
welcoming us to heaven.
This is Good News, my friend!

ARTHUR O. ROBERTS

Biblical References to Resurrection and Eternal Life

Listed below are selected scriptural passages on the subjects of resurrection and eternal life. All passages are quoted from the New Revised Standard Version.

RESURRECTION

Luke 14:14 And you will be blessed, because they cannot repay you, for you will be repaid at the resurrection of the righteous.

Luke 20:27–35 Some Sadducees, those who say there is no resurrection, came to him and asked him a question, "Teacher, Moses wrote for us that if a man's brother dies, leaving a wife but no children, the man shall marry the widow and raise up children for his brother. . . . In the resurrection, therefore, whose wife will the woman be?" . . . Jesus said to them, ". . . [T]hose who are considered worthy of a place in that age and in the resurrection from the dead neither marry nor are given in marriage."

Luke 20:36 Indeed they cannot die anymore, because they are like angels and are children of God, being children of the resurrection.

John 5:28–29 [F]or the hour is coming when all who are in their graves will hear his voice and will come out—those who have done good, to the resurrection of life, and those who have done evil, to the resurrection of condemnation.

John 11:24 Martha said to him, "I know that he will rise again in the resurrection on the last day." Jesus said to her, "I am the resurrection and the life. Those who believe in me, even though they die, will live."

Acts 1:21–22 So one of the men who have accompanied us during all the time that the Lord Jesus went in and out among us, beginning from the baptism of John until the day when he was taken up from us—one of these must become a witness with us to his resurrection.

Acts 2:31 Foreseeing this, David spoke of the resurrection of the Messiah, saying, "He was not abandoned to Hades, nor did his flesh experience corruption."

Acts 4:2 The Sadducees came to them, much annoyed because they were teaching the people and proclaiming that in Jesus there is the resurrection of the dead.

Acts 4:33 With great power the apostles gave their testimony to the resurrection of the Lord Jesus, and great grace was upon them all.

Acts 17:18 Also some Epicurean and Stoic philosophers debated with him. Some said, "What does this babbler want to say?" Others said, "He seems to be a proclaimer of foreign divinities." (This was because he was telling the good news about Jesus and the resurrection.)

Acts 17:32 When they heard of the resurrection of the dead, some scoffed; but others said, "We will hear you again about this."

Acts 23:6 When Paul noticed that some were Sadducees and others were Pharisees, he called out in the council, "Brothers, I am a Pharisee, a son of Pharisees. I am on trial concerning the hope of the resurrection of the dead."

Acts 23:8 (The Sadducees say that there is no resurrection, or angel, or spirit; but the Pharisees acknowledge all three.)

Acts 24:15 I have a hope in God—a hope that they themselves also accept—that there will be a resurrection of both the righteous and the unrighteous.

Acts 24:20–21 Or let these men here tell what crime they had found when I stood before the council, unless it was this one sentence that I called out while standing before them, "It is about the resurrection of the dead that I am on trial before you today."

Rom. 1:3–4 . . . the gospel concerning his Son, who was descended from David according to the flesh and was declared to be Son of God with power according to the spirit of holiness by resurrection from the dead, Jesus Christ our Lord.

Rom. 6:5 For if we have been united with him in a death like his, we will certainly be united with him in a resurrection like his.

1 Cor. 15:12 Now if Christ is proclaimed as raised from the dead, how can some of you say there is no resurrection of the dead? If there is no resurrection of the dead, then Christ has not been raised.

1 Cor. 15:21 For since death came through a human being, the resurrection of the dead has also come through a human being.

1 Cor. 15:42 So it is with the resurrection of the dead. What is sown is perishable, what is raised is imperishable.

Phil. 3:10 I want to know Christ and the power of his resurrection and the sharing of his sufferings by becoming like him in his death, if somehow I may attain the resurrection from the dead.

2 Tim. 2:17–18 Among them are Hymenaeus and Philetus, who have swerved from the truth by claiming that the resurrection has already taken place. They are upsetting the faith of some.

Heb. 6:1–2 Therefore let us go on toward perfection, leaving behind the basic teaching about Christ, and not laying again the foundation: repentance from dead works and faith toward God, instruction about baptisms, laying on of hands, resurrection of the dead, and eternal judgment.

Heb. 11:35 Women received their dead by resurrection. Others were tortured, refusing to accept release, in order to obtain a better resurrection.

1 Pet. 1:3 Blessed be the God and Father of our Lord Jesus Christ! By his great mercy he has given us a new birth into a living hope through the resurrection of Jesus Christ from the dead.

1 Pet. 3:21 And baptism, which this prefigured, now saves you—not as a removal of dirt from the body, but as an appeal to God for a good conscience, through the resurrection of Jesus Christ.

Rev. 20:5 (The rest of the dead did not come to life until the thousand years were ended.) This is the first resurrection.

Rev. 20:6 Blessed and holy are those who share in the first resurrection. Over these the second death has no power, but they will be priests of God and of Christ, and they will reign with him a thousand years.

ETERNAL LIFE

Wisdom of Sol. 2:23–3:1 God created us for incorruption, and made us in the image of his own eternity, but through the devil's envy death entered the world, and those who belong to his company experience it. But the souls of the righteous are in the hand of God, and no torment will ever touch them.

Matt. 19:29 And everyone who has left houses or brothers or sisters or father or mother or children or fields for my sake will receive a hundred times as much and will inherit eternal life.

Matt. 25:46 And these will go away into eternal punishment, but the righteous into eternal life.

Mark 10:17 As he was setting out on a journey, a man ran up and knelt before him, and asked him, "Good Teacher, what must I do to inherit eternal life?"

Mark 10:29–30 Jesus said, "Truly I tell you, there is no one who has left house or brothers or sisters or mother or father or children or fields, for my sake and for the sake of the good news, who will not receive a hundredfold now in this age (houses, brothers and sisters, mothers and children, and fields with persecutions) and in the age to come eternal life."

Luke 10:25–28 Just then a lawyer stood up to test Jesus. "Teacher," he said, "what must I do to inherit eternal life?" He said to him, "What is written in the law? What do you read there?" He answered, "You shall love the Lord your God with all your heart, and with all your soul, and with all your strength, and with all your mind; and your neighbor as yourself." And he said to him, "You have given the right answer; do this, and you will live."

Luke 18:18 A certain ruler asked him, "Good Teacher, what must I do to inherit eternal life?"

Luke 18:29–30 And he said to them, "Truly I tell you, there is no one who has left house or wife or brothers or parents or children, for the sake of the kingdom of God, who will not get back very much more in this age, and in the age to come eternal life."

John 3:14–16 And just as Moses lifted up the serpent in the wilderness, so must the Son of Man be lifted up, that whoever believes in him may have eternal life. "For God so loved the world that he gave his only Son, so that everyone who believes in him may not perish but may have eternal life."

John 3:36 Whoever believes in the Son has eternal life; whoever disobeys the Son will not see life, but must endure God's wrath.

John 4:13–14 Jesus said to her, "Everyone who drinks of this water will be thirsty again, but those who drink of the water that I will give them will never be thirsty. The water that I will give will become in them a spring of water gushing up to eternal life."

John 4:36 The reaper is already receiving wages and is gathering fruit for eternal life, so that sower and reaper may rejoice together.

John 5:24 Very truly, I tell you, anyone who hears my word and believes him who sent me has eternal life, and does not come under judgment, but has passed from death to life.

John 5:39–40 "You search the scriptures because you think that in them you have eternal life; and it is they that testify on my behalf. Yet you refuse to come to me to have life."

John 6:27 Do not work for the food that perishes, but for the food that endures for eternal life, which the Son of Man will give you. For it is on him that God the Father has set his seal.

John 6:40 This is indeed the will of my Father, that all who see the Son and believe in him may have eternal life; and I will raise them up on the last day.

John 6:54 Those who eat my flesh and drink my blood have eternal life, and I will raise them up on the last day.

John 6:68 Simon Peter answered him, "Lord, to whom can we go? You have the words of eternal life."

John 10:28 I give them eternal life, and they will never perish. No one will snatch them out of my hand.

John 12:25 Those who love their life lose it, and those who hate their life in this world will keep it for eternal life.

John 12:50 And I know that his commandment is eternal life. What I speak, therefore, I speak just as the Father has told me.

John 17:1–3 After Jesus had spoken these words, he looked up to heaven and said, "Father, the hour has come; glorify your Son so that the Son may glorify you, since you have given him authority over all people, to give eternal life to all whom you have given him. And this is eternal life, that they may know you, the only true God, and Jesus Christ whom you have sent."

Acts 13:46–7 Then both Paul and Barnabas spoke out boldly, saying, "It was necessary that the word of God should be spoken first to you. Since you reject it and judge yourselves to be unworthy of eternal life, we are now turning to the Gentiles. For so the Lord has commanded us, saying, 'I have set you to be a light for the Gentiles, so that you may bring salvation to the ends of the earth.'"

Rom. 2:6–7 For he will repay according to each one's deeds: to those who by patiently doing good seek for glory and honor and immortality, he will give eternal life.

Rom. 5:20–21 But law came in, with the result that the trespass multiplied; but where sin increased, grace abounded all the more, so that, just as sin exercised dominion in death, so grace might also exercise dominion through justification leading to eternal life through Jesus Christ our Lord.

Rom. 6:21–23 So what advantage did you then get from the things of which you now are ashamed? The end of those things is death. But now that you have been freed from sin and enslaved to God, the advantage you get is sanctification. The end is eternal life. For the wages of sin is death, but the free gift of God is eternal life in Christ Jesus our Lord.

2 Cor. 4:16–5:5: So we do not lose heart. Even though our outer nature is wasting away, our inner nature is being renewed day by day. For this slight momentary affliction is preparing us for an eternal weight of glory beyond all measure, because we look not at what can be seen but at what cannot be seen; for what can be seen is temporary, but what cannot be seen is eternal. For we know that if the earthly tent we live in is destroyed, we have a building from God, a house not made with hands, eternal in the heavens. For in this tent we groan, longing to be clothed with our heavenly dwelling—if indeed, when we have taken it off we will not be found naked. For while we are still in this tent, we groan under our burden, because we wish not to be unclothed but to be further clothed, so

that what is mortal may be swallowed up by life. He who has prepared us for this very thing is God, who has given us the Spirit as a guarantee.

Gal. 6:8 If you sow to your own flesh, you will reap corruption from the flesh; but if you sow to the Spirit, you will reap eternal life from the Spirit.

1 Tim. 1:16 But for that very reason I received mercy, so that in me, as the foremost, Jesus Christ might display the utmost patience, making me an example to those who would come to believe in him for eternal life.

1 Tim. 6:12 Fight the good fight of the faith; take hold of the eternal life, to which you were called and for which you made the good confession in the presence of many witnesses.

Titus 1:1–2 Paul, a servant of God and an apostle of Jesus Christ, for the sake of the faith of God's elect and the knowledge of the truth that is in accordance with godliness, in the hope of eternal life that God, who never lies, promised before the ages began.

Titus 3:6–7 This Spirit he poured out on us richly through Jesus Christ our Savior, so that, having been justified by his grace, we might become heirs according to the hope of eternal life.

1 John 1:1–2 We declare to you what was from the beginning, what we have heard, what we have seen with our eyes, what we have looked at and touched with our hands, concerning the word of life—this life was revealed, and we have seen it and testify to it, and declare to you the eternal life that was with the Father and was revealed to us.

1 John 2:25 And this is what he has promised us, eternal life.

1 John 3:15 All who hate a brother or sister are murderers, and you know that murderers do not have eternal life abiding in them.

1 John 5:11–13 And this is the testimony: God gave us eternal life, and this life is in his Son. Whoever has the Son has life; whoever does not have the Son of God does not have life. I write these things to you who believe in the name of the Son of God, so that you may know that you have eternal life.

1 John 5:20 And we know that the Son of God has come and has given us understanding so that we may know him who is true; and we are in him who is true, in his Son Jesus Christ. He is the true God and eternal life.

Jude 21 Keep yourselves in the love of God; look forward to the mercy of our Lord Jesus Christ that leads to eternal life.

General William Booth Enters into Heaven

By Vachel Lindsay

[To be sung to the tune of "The Blood of the Lamb"
with indicated instrument]

[Bass drum beaten loudly.]
Booth led boldly with his big bass drum—
(Are you washed in the blood of the Lamb?)
The Saints smiled gravely and they said: "He's come."
(Are you washed in the blood of the Lamb?)
Walking lepers followed, rank on rank,
Lurching bravoes from the ditches dank,
Drabs from the alleyways and drug fiends pale—
Minds still passion-ridden, soul-powers frail:—
Vermin-eaten saints with mouldy breath,
Unwashed legions with the ways of Death—
(Are you washed in the blood of the Lamb?)

[Banjos.]
Every slum had sent its half-a-score
The round world over. (Booth had groaned for more.)
Every banner that the wide world flies
Bloomed with glory and transcendent dyes.
Big-voiced lasses made their banjos bang,
Tranced, fanatical they shrieked and sang:—
"Are you washed in the blood of the Lamb?"
Hallelujah! It was queer to see
Bull-necked convicts with that land make free.
Loons with trumpets blowed a blare, blare, blare
On, on upward thro' the golden air!
(Are you washed in the blood of the Lamb?)

[Bass drum slower and softer.]
Booth died blind and still by Faith he trod,
Eyes still dazzled by the ways of God.
Booth led boldly, and he looked the chief
Eagle countenance in sharp relief,
Beard a-flying, air of high command
Unabated in that holy land.

[Sweet flute music.]
Jesus came from out the court-house door,
Stretched his hands above the passing poor.
Booth saw not, but led his queer ones there
Round and round the mighty court-house square.
Yet in an instant all that blear review
Marched on spotless, clad in raiment new.
The lame were straightened, withered limbs uncurled
And blind eyes opened on a new, sweet world.

[Bass drum louder.]
Drabs and vixens in a flash made whole!
Gone was the weasel head, the snout, the jowl!
Sages and sibyls now, and athletes clean,
Rulers of empires, and of forests green!

[Grand chorus of all instruments. Tambourines to the foreground.]
The hosts were sandalled, and their wings were fire!
(Are you washed in the blood of the Lamb?)
But their noise played havoc with the angel-choir.
(Are you washed in the blood of the Lamb?)
O, shout Salvation! It was good to see
Kings and Princes by the Lamb set free.
The banjos rattled and the tambourines
Jing-jing-jingled in the hands of Queens.

[Reverently sung, no instruments.]
And when Booth halted by the curb for prayer
He saw his Master thro' the flag-filled air.
Christ came gently with a robe and crown
For Booth the soldier, while the throng knelt down.
He saw King Jesus. They were face to face,
And he knelt a-weeping in that holy place.
Are you washed in the blood of the Lamb?[*]

---

[*] Vachel Lindsay's poem "General William Booth Enters into Heaven" has appeared in various collections, including the work from which this poem was taken, *The Congo and Other Poems* (Macmillan, 1915). I have used an early text in an Internet collection, *The Poets' Corner* (www.poets'-corner.org).

ANNOTATED
BIBLIOGRAPHY

The works included in this Annotated Bibliography all deal, in varying ways, with the subject of heaven. (Please note that not all sources named in the endnotes appear in this annotated list.)

Allen, Diogenes. *Christian Belief in a Postmodern World: The Full Wealth of Conviction.* Louisville, KY: Fortress/Knox Press, 1989. A Princeton theologian offers a contemporary apologetic for the Christian faith. Chap. 9, "Divine Agency in a Scientific World," is particularly germane to the topic of heaven. Discussing the interface of human freedom and divine agency, Allen writes: "God does not have a blueprint for history or for individual lives. Rather, God interacts with human agents, seeking to realize God's intentions for them without violating their freedom" (p. 178).

Augustine. *Confessions and Enchiridion.* Vol. 7 of the *Library of Christian Classics (LCC).* Translated and edited by Albert C. Outler. Philadelphia, PA: Westminster Press, 1955. Augustine deals concretely with the resurrection in chap. 23 of the *Enchiridion.* He holds firmly to a bodily resurrection, anticipating "wholeness for the self" and "an equality of physical endowment." Augustine finds "spiritual body" well-matched with "fleshly body" *(corpus spirituale* versus *corpus animale);* the term is not for him an oxymoron, but a way to signify recreated wholeness. God—"an artist who works in marvelous and mysterious ways—will restore our bodies" (pp. 390–394).

Barbour, Ian G. *Religion and Science: Historical and Contemporary Issues*. San Francisco: HarperSanFrancisco, 1997. Revised and expanded edition of *Religion in an Age of Science* (1990). This is an excellent summary of issues facing both scientists and theologians who seek to understand the mysteries of the universe and its Creator, by a scholar instrumental in bridging the chasm between scientific and theological understandings of the universe. Barbour explicates how Christ the Word is understood biblically as active in both creation and redemption and, if life exists on other planets, is active there, too (p. 215).

Barth, Karl. *Church Dogmatics*. Edinburgh, UK: Clark, 1936–1969. Vol. 3.3: *Doctrine of Creation*. Heaven, said Barth, is distinct from earth; it allows for God to be in dialogue with man and provides a plurality of creatures (p. 453). About its elusiveness he wrote: "[T]he unknown is not as such unknowable. But the unknowable waits at the limits of the knowable" (p. 424).

Baxter, Richard. *The Saints' Everlasting Rest*. Abridged by Benjamin Fawcett. Kidderminster, UK, 1758. Reprint, New York: The American Tract Society, n.d. Published first in 1650, this book was a major Puritan contribution to the subject of the afterlife. The title is drawn from Heb. 4:9: "There remaineth therefore a rest unto the people of God" (KJV). To persecuted people rest signifies more than it does to folks who are merely tired. Baxter defines heavenly rest thus: "the perfect, endless enjoyment of God by the perfected saints, according to the measure of their capacity, to which their souls arrive at death, and both soul and body most fully after the resurrection and final judgment" (p. 17). Although the book consists mainly of exhortations to spiritual disciplines to prepare for the afterlife, or to reach the unconverted, certain chapters deal with the nature of the heavenly life—particularly joys at being immediately with God eternally, without the impediment of sin. Baxter emphasizes the greatly enhanced nature of both body and soul, and the perfection of human society when sin no longer intrudes.

Berkouwer, G. C. *The Return of Christ*. Grand Rapids, MI: Eerdmans, 1972. Using biblical exegesis the author shows "earthly" and "spiritual" to be complementary not contradictory descriptions of reality. He writes:

"The opinion that the themes of the new earth and the vision of God are competitive can only stem from an unbiblical idea of God's glory that relativizes or even eliminates concern for *things* and *mankind*" (p. 227). It will be on earth, he adds, citing Rev. 22:17, "that the voice will sound 'let him who is thirsty come, let him who desires take the water of life without price'" (p. 234).

Bonhoeffer, Dietrich. *The Martyred Christian*. Edited by Joan Winmill Brown. New York: Macmillan, 1983. A famous martyred member of the German Confessional Church during World War II writes, "Wherever it is recognized that the power of death has been broken, wherever the world of death is illumined by the miracle of the resurrection and of new life . . . one neither clings convulsively to life nor casts it frivolously away. One is content with the allotted span and one does not invest earthly things with the title of eternity" (p. 209).

Brin, David. *Brightness Reef*. New York: Bantam Books, 1995. This contemporary science fiction writer's vision of immortality is that of intelligence guiding evolution down long stretches of time—billions of years—and across galactic space.

Buechner, Frederick. *Wishful Thinking: A Seeker's ABC*. Revised and expanded edition. San Francisco: HarperSanFrancisco, 1993. In topical format this minister discusses theological topics in everyday words. His section on "Immortality" includes this statement: "All the major Christian creeds affirm belief in resurrection *of the body*. In other words, they affirm the belief that what God in spite of everything prizes enough to bring back to life is not just some disembodied echo of human beings but a new and revised version of all things which made them the particular human beings they were and which they need something like a body to express: their personality, the way they looked, the sound of their voices, their peculiar capacity for creating and loving, in some sense their *faces*" (p. 51).

Calvin, John. *Institutes of the Christian Religion*. Philadelphia, PA: Westminster, 1955. See especially book 3, chap. 25. This sixteenth-century Reformed theologian emphasizes two scriptural teachings that help overcome difficulty in believing that a dead body can be resurrected: "one in the parallel of Christ's resurrection; the other in the omnipotence of God" (book 3, chap. 25, p. 990). He examines scriptural texts in support of a physical resurrection. We will have the same bodies, not different ones, he asserts. He feels that our intelligence is incapable of detailing that mystery and cautions against over-speculation.

Carter, Jimmy. *Always a Reckoning and Other Poems.* New York: Times Books, 1995. A former United States president (in retirement an active participant in Habitat for Humanity) has written several books bearing oblique Christian witness—among them, this book of poems.

Clarke, Arthur C. *3001: The Final Odyssey.* New York: Del Rey, 1997. A creative science fiction author offers this secular soliloquy about the human future: "Whatever godlike powers and principalities lurked beyond the stars, Poole reminded himself, for ordinary humans only two things were important: Love and Death. His body had not yet aged a hundred years: he still had plenty of time for both" (pp. 245–246).

The Classics of Western Spirituality (CWS). New York: Paulist Press. Of the 100 volumes presently in this comprehensive series, several books offer helpful reading on this subject—among them, the following:

> Angela of Foligno. *Complete Works* (*CWS* 1993). This thirteenth-century mystic and friend of Francis wrote of five mysteries about Christ. The first is divine love, the second is the certitude of salvation given us through the incarnation, the third is Jesus' death, which procured our salvation, the fourth is Jesus' resurrection, which gives us "a firm hope" of our own, and the fifth is the ascension, bringing completion to salvation (see pp. 309–310).

> Angeles Silesius (Johann Scheffler). *The Cherubinic Wanderer* (*CWS* 1986). This seventeenth-century book contains many delightful couplets, such as this: "Heaven humbles itself, toward earth makes its descent; When will the earth arise and become heaven-bent?" (p. 73).

> *Apocalyptic Spirituality* (*CWS* 1979). This volume includes writings from Lactantius, Joachim of Fiore, and Savonarola, whose pictures of heaven are filled with precious-stone imagery and levels of perfection.

Celtic Spirituality (*CWS* 1999). Celtic Christianity preserved an earthiness less influenced by Greek thought than the early Western church generally. "The Vision of Adamnán" narrates the author's ecstatic transport into the next world. Adamnán is given a tour by angels, first into the rabble-filled realms of hell and then into glorious "lands of the Saints." Heaven is protected from evil by a ring of fire and ice, which the blessed ones are allowed to pass through. In Adamnán's vision the saints come from north and south, east and west to gather about the glorious throne of God and sing praises. Children and birds surround Mary and the apostles and join in the singing. Hell is the home of the devil and the demons, who torment the damned by dunking them in rivers of fire, snow, poison, and muck. In contrast, the redeemed enjoy a realm "without pride or arrogance, without untruth or misdeed, without deception or penitence, without aggression or shame or disgrace, without reproach or envy, without haughtiness, without sickness or disease, without poverty or nakedness, without death or extinction, without hail or snow, without wind or rain, without noise or thunder, without darkness or cold. It is a fine, wonderful, delightful realm, filled with fruit and light and the fragrance of a perfect land in which every excellence is enjoyed" (section 4, pp. 330ff).

Maneri, Sharafuddin. *The Hundred Letters* (*CWS* 1980). See especially letters 27 and 100. This major Sufi writer gives an Islamic interpretation of heaven that ranges from earthy to ethereal. The blessed will praise the Lord for eight hundred thousand years, Maneri says. The first stage of paradise is "filled with beautiful damsels, mansions, streams, trees and purified wine." This is an accommodation to earthly minded people for whom hell is prepared, mercifully, for those who persist after lusts. But the second stage offers the "Gift beyond description" and the "Wealth that eludes the imagination." The third stage offers union with the "Friend," with no limits placed on the expanse of the heavenly dwelling place. "Compared to the refreshment of union, heaven is a pile of rubbish: In the path of lovers, it looms as a trivial gain!" (p. 108).

Native Mesoamerican Spirituality (*CWS* 1980). This work includes many rituals about life and death, sayings of the sages, philosophical reflections, and considerable poetry, some of which expresses poignantly a longing for an eternal home. The volume, edited by Miguel Leon-Portilla, preserves some material from various indigenous languages and reflects the culture of the people who lived in much of what is now Mexico and adjacent parts of Central America, particularly during a period from the tenth to the sixteenth centuries A.D.

Nicolas of Cusa. *On Learned Ignorance* (*CWS* 1997). This fifteenth-century scholar says that in Jesus is a "true union of soul and body" (p. 187). Jesus is the center and circumference of intellectual nature. His resurrection is our pattern. Where he is as an ascended being is beyond sadness and suffering and other aspects of temporality. "And we must speak of this place of eternal joy and peace as above the heavens, although with reference to place it is not apprehensible, describable, or definable" (p. 191).

Origen. *An Exhortation to Martyrdom, Prayer and Selected Works* (*CWS* 1979). Origen found allegorical meanings in scriptural events. For example, in the journeys of the Israelites as recorded in the book of Numbers, the name-places become soul-stages; and the Song of Solomon depicts divine-human love. Although admitting a first level of meaning in narrative (that is, the facts), he assumes that the deeper meanings are the treasures "hidden in the field." Progress is from the material to the immaterial, the corporal to the incorporeal (see pp. 198ff). Concerning humanity stamped with the divine image, Origen interprets the *imago Dei* to refer not to the body which decays, but rather to "the intelligence of the soul, its righteousness, temperance, courage, wisdom, discipline and through the entire chorus of virtues that are present in God by substance, and can be in man through effort and by imitation" (p. 216). Origen's views reflect Platonic philosophy and contrast considerably with those of Tertullian.

Philo of Alexandria, *The Contemplative Life* (and other writings) (*CWS* 1981). This Jewish scholar, who lived from 20 B.C. to 50 A.D., believed in souls, demons, and angels. In his view souls of philosophers spurn the physical to become part of the immaterial, the immortal. Heaven is "eternal day," the superior part of the cosmos (p. 108). "The soul experiences its most vigorous flowering of knowledge when the body's prime is withering away through length of years. So it is a hard fate to be tripped up by the heels before one has attained one's prime" (p. 148).

Swedenborg, Emanuel. *The Universal Human and Soul-Body Interaction* (*CWS* 1980). Edited and translated by George F. Dole. Introduction by Stephen Larsen; preface by Robert Kirven. This complex work elaborates a theory of nature and super-nature linked in "correspondences." In special visions, says Swedenborg, he has been shown heaven and hell, which he describes in colorful detail. To many readers this book is a unique and somewhat baffling blend of fantasy and insight about the role of the body in the realm of the spirit.

Conyers, A. J. *The Eclipse of Heaven.* Downers Grove, IL: InterVarsity Press, 1992. The author laments that the world no longer views heaven as an overarching context for life on earth. Catastrophes and social upheavals are viewed from secular perspectives. To weigh events against transcendent glory, in his judgment, is necessary for a true understanding of love and passion in this life.

Csikszentmihalyi, Mihaly. *The Evolving Self: a Psychology for the Third Millennium.* New York: HarperCollins, 1993. This book is a well-articulated exposition of secular hope. The author thinks that evolution is now under human control through our genes and memes (cultural units), and that this mastery augurs well for the future, despite obstacles and setbacks.

Cullman, Oscar. *Immortality of the Soul or Resurrection of the Body?* London: Epworth, 1958. Cullman considers the coming of Christ the central event in history and affirms the resurrection as a real occurrence. The deliverance of the cosmos from its bondage to sin "will come when the power of the Holy Spirit transforms all matter" (p. 37).

David. The ancient Hebrew poet/king extols the Creator in many psalms. He understands the need for awe before the creation and for humanity's responsibility to be stewards of it. This biblical concept of dominion has irritated some people, who feel it has been used to rationalize human exploitation of other species. That exploitation has occurred doesn't excuse humanity from responsibility as stewards; rather, it holds them to it. Faithfulness arises from an appropriate awe before the Almighty. Psalm 8 illustrates a theistic foundation for true dominion:

> O LORD, our Sovereign, how majestic is your name in all the earth! You have set your glory above the heavens. Out of the mouths of babes and infants you have founded a bulwark because of your foes, to silence the enemy and the avenger. When I look at your heavens, the work of your fingers, the moon and the stars that you have established; what are human beings that you are mindful of them, mortals that you care for them? Yet you have made them a little lower than God, and crowned them with glory and honor. You have given them dominion over the works of your hands; you have put all things under their feet, all sheep and oxen, and also the beasts of the field, the birds of the air, and the fish of the sea, whatever passes along the paths of the seas.

Davis, Stephen T. *Risen Indeed: Making Sense of the Resurrection.* Grand Rapids, MI: Eerdmans, 1993. In this book a philosopher from Claremont McKenna College shows the logic of Jesus' resurrection. In the tradition of the early church fathers Davis offers a finely reasoned apologetic for historic, orthodox Christianity. He supports a body-soul dualism; but he also believes that "the Christian view of the resurrection is viable even on a materialist or physicalist basis" (p. 110). About persons in hell Davis writes, "[T]hey are in hell because they chose to be" (p. 155).

Dewart, Joanne E. McWilliams. *Death and Resurrection.* Wilmington, DE: Glazier, 1986. Vol. 22 of *The Message of the Fathers of the Church.* A compilation of thoughts on the subject by early Christian scholars.

Ellul, Jacques. *The Meaning of the City.* Grand Rapids, MI: Eerdmans, 1970. A classic study that adapts for modern readers the theme of Augustine's influential treatise *The City of God.* Ellul is perceptive about the significance of symbols found within the biblical book of Revelation.

The End of the World and the Ends of God: Science and Theology on Eschatology. Edited by John Polkinghorne and Michael Welker. Harrisburg, PA: Trinity Press, 2000. This volume includes helpful essays by several scientists and theologians. Miroslav Volf's outstanding concluding essay, "Enter into Joy," probes several important issues, including the last judgment as rooted in God's grace, and time within eternity. Changes for creatures as they move from earth to heaven aren't limited to measurements linear or circular, Volf writes, but can also be construed as "kaleidoscopic (as a child's play may be described)" (p. 270). I'm much indebted to this work and to writings by Polkinghorne himself (noted below), which bridge an unfortunate and needless chasm between science and theology.

Evidence of Purpose. Edited by John Marks Templeton. New York: Continuum, 1994. This is a book of essays by ten Christian scholars who believe that scientific inquiry is compatible with divine purpose. Harvard astronomer Owen Gingerich provides a well-reasoned essay on the evidence of purpose in the cosmos. British scientist-theologian Arthur Peacocke reflects upon God and time. He writes: "God is eternal, in the sense that there is no time at which he did not exist nor will there be a future time at which he does not exist" (p. 103).

Fackre, Gabriel. *The Christian Story.* Revised edition. Grand Rapids, MI: Eerdmans, 1984. The chapter on "Consummation" emphasizes everlasting life as reconciliation, with God, with humanity, with nature. His "visionary realism" recognizes that human advancement on earth, so integral to Christian witness, is "plagued with ambiguity," but Christian hope resists cynicism. He writes: "While perceiving the shadows ahead in the corridor of the future, it knows that Jesus Christ has torn down the 'No Exit' sign at its end and shouldered open its dark door" (p. 249).

Four Views of Hell. Edited by William Crockett. Grand Rapids, MI: Zondervan, 1992. The four views delineated and discussed thoughtfully are: literal, metaphysical, purgatorial, and conditional.

Gilmore, John. *Probing Heaven: Key Questions.* Grand Rapids, MI: Baker Book House, 1989 and 1993. A helpful book that uses a question-answer format. Regarding time in eternity, Gilmore espouses a "stand still" or "present time" view, rather than endless duration; but he admits its paradoxical aspects. On the question of growth in heaven, the author offers pros and cons. He indicates that some theologians posit a perfection that cannot admit of improvement, while others argue for continued growth of understanding. Here is his summary: "We have presented the opinion that the finalization of heaven has no limits to continued growth" (p. 294).

Graham, Billy. *Angels: God's Secret Agents.* New York: Doubleday, 1975. A much-admired Christian evangelist details numerous instances, biblical or otherwise, of angels appearing on the human scene, mostly to help or protect human beings. Angels, he holds, are nonmaterial spirits, and there are millions of them. They're able to appear in human form if sent from God. He believes that an ancient rebellion of Lucifer led to a major, ongoing cosmic war, which will end with the triumph of Christ. Graham urges believers to be more open to angelic messengers of the Lord, inasmuch as nonbelieving culture has demonstrated a tragic fascination with the demonic spirits. He writes: "In contrast to Jesus, we all still have to die. Yet just as an angel was involved in Christ's resurrection, so will angels help us in death. Only one thin veil separates our natural world from the spiritual world. That thin veil we call death. However, Christ both vanquished death and overcame the dark threats of the evil fallen angels" (p. 148).

Greene, Brian. *The Elegant Universe.* New York: Vintage Books, 1999. This physicist expounds a "string theory" of the universe, and ponders whether our universe is just a tiny part of a larger "multiverse." He combines solid scientific exegesis with humble wonder. "The history of science teaches us," he writes, "that each time we think we have it all figured out, nature has a radical surprise in store for us that requires significant and sometimes drastic changes in how we think the world works" (p. 373). Greene envisions each generation building upon previous ones more fully to comprehend the cosmos. He doesn't write from a theological perspective about this scientific search for "the ultimate theory," but his openness to new revelations of truth is not incompatible with a theistic view of a vastly altered cosmos.

Habermas, Gary R., and J. P. Moreland. *Beyond Death: Exploring the Evidence for Immortality.* Wheaton, IL: Crossway, 1998. With a careful attention to boundaries of logic, the authors argue the evidence for, the nature of, and the implications of immortality. They show that the Christian view of life after death is credible, and that attempts to discount, or explain away, the resurrection of Jesus fail. The authors provide a useful summary of near-death experiences from their own observations and from the observations and research of Kübler-Ross, Moody, and other recent writers. They devote only a few pages to the nature of the heavenly experience. In sum they consider that heaven will be a substantial place for embodied persons, that negative qualities will be absent (pain, sorrow, etc.), and that the glorified state will not be boring.

Hall, Pearl Crist. *Long Road to Freedom: One Person's Discovery of Death.* Richmond, IN: Friends United Press, 1978. The author and her husband were social activists who in later life discovered a dimension of spirituality that had been missing in their preoccupation with justice. "That Power that splits open a buried acorn and pushes up an oak tree," she writes, "that Creative Force that contrives a butterfly from a dull cocoon and sets a winged creature spinning in a new milieu, that Innate Energy that cracks a thin eggshell and sends forth a bird with a song unheard before, such a Dynamic can be trusted to break this body's box and let the soul spill out in a transformed creativity" (p. 95). There will be no sting after death, for "anticipated revelation becomes genuine experience. Such awareness is beyond the present, and all that has been seen as through a glass darkly now shines of true life and with whatever splendor, compassion, truth and wisdom God holds for me" (p. 100).

Hallett, Garth L. "The Tedium of Immortality," *Faith and Philosophy,* vol. 18, no. 3, July 2001. He answers people's fear that they would be bored in heaven and recommends we take a tip from the mystics, so enraptured with God nothing could ever seem drab or monotonous.

Harvard Divinity Bulletin, vols. 29 and 30, 2000 and 2001–2002. These contain the Ingersoll lectures by Carol Zaleski and Huston Smith. The Ingersoll series deals with questions of immortality from major scholars representing various viewpoints. The Harvard Divinity School maintains an archive of the lectures in a series that has continued for more than a century.

Hebblethwaite, Brian. *The Incarnation: Collected Essays in Christology.* New York: Cambridge Press, 1987. This author contrasts the "inspirational" view of Jesus, wherein Jesus inspires us in various ways, with the "incarnational" view of Jesus. He affirms the latter. The former view, he avers, misses the central Christian message, turning it into just another religion. (I might add that in respect to heaven the incarnational view offers realistic re-creation of the cosmos instead of merely enhanced qualities of earthly life.)

How Different Religions View Death and Afterlife. Edited by C. J. Johnson and M. G. McGee. Philadelphia, PA: Charles Press, 1998. Scholars from A to Z (Assemblies of God to Zoroastrianism) offer summaries of their views and give brief answers to questions posed by the editors. (I myself wrote the section depicting the Quaker view of death and the afterlife.)

Irenaeus of Lyons. *Against Heresies.* In *Early Christian Fathers,* vol. 1 of the *Library of Christian Classics.* Philadelphia, PA: Westminster, 1953. A second-century Christian scholar affirms the full humanity of Christ and the resurrection of real persons. He anticipates variety in the afterlife, believing that some people will dwell in the different regions of the heavens, some in rural paradise, others in the city—an extrapolation from the parable of the sower and the seed (Matt. 13), hundredfold, sixtyfold, thirtyfold. People won't grow old, but "always remain new, in converse with God" (p. 396).

James, P. D. *Death in Holy Orders.* New York: Ballantine Books, 2001. In this work of fiction an astute mystery writer ponders theological mysteries, including the resurrection of Jesus. The villain in the plot, Gregory, epitomizes cynicism and its immoral consequences in an age of unbelief. Christianity has become irrelevant and the church is dying, he asserts. This is his analysis: "If life is hard and short and full of pain, you need the hope of heaven; if there is no effective law, you need the deterrent of hell. The Church gave them pictures and stories and the hope of everlasting life." Gregory then lists alternatives in the twenty-first century that fulfill people's need for myth and ritual: football, art, music, the Internet, pornography, etc. "We all have our own resources for staving off those two horrors of human life, boredom and the knowledge that we die," he declares. When a character named Emma asks what Gregory will do if these things fail, he replies, "Then, my dear, I shall turn to science" for a quick death (p. 281). Gregory is depicted by the author as a fallen son of light—like Lucifer. The novel's plot affirms the Christian hope.

Jesus' Resurrection: Fact or Fiction. Edited by Paul Copan and Roland K. Tacelli. Downers Grove, IL: InterVarsity Press, 2000. This is a scholarly debate between believers and nonbelievers. It raises major evidentiary issues. For believers Robert Gundry and Stephen Davis, it constitutes a contemporary apologetic, the sort of writing early Christian philosophers such as Justin, Athenagoras, and Tertullian provided to convince a skeptical Greco-Roman audience of the credibility of the Christian faith.

Jewett, Paul. *God, Creation, and Revelation.* Grand Rapids, MI: Eerdmans, 1991. Heaven, writes Jewett, "describes not only the visible realm of time and space, but the invisible realm where saints and angels enjoy fellowship with the Creator beyond the reach of sin and death" (p. 469).

Justin Martyr. "Fragments of the Lost Work of Justin on the Resurrection." Translated by M. Dods. Vol. 1 of *Ante-Nicene Christian Fathers.* Grand Rapids, MI: Christian Classics Ethereal Library (Internet version), 2002. This second-century philosopher affirms the credibility of Christianity generally and the resurrection of the body specifically. He affirms the wholeness of persons, physical, mental, and supremely spiritual.

Kreeft, Peter. *Angels (and Demons).* San Francisco, CA: Ignatius Press, 1995. In a popular format, the author poses and answers 100 questions people have asked about angels (and demons). Sample question (#25): "Do we become angels when we die?" Answer: "No. We don't change species."

———. *Heaven: The Heart's Deepest Longing.* San Francisco, CA: Ignatius Press, 1989. Kreeft accepts as credible testimony the diffuse but insistent human longing for heaven as the true home. He shows how the present world is infused with divine purpose, its joys and hopes offering cues to eternal life. Kreeft elaborates his views vis-à-vis various philosophical questions. He includes C. S. Lewis's *Weight of Glory* and other excerpts in an appendix. Kreeft asserts three things we know about heaven: First, "it is more real, more substantial," than earth; second, "heaven has more dimensions than earth, not fewer"; and third, "heaven is clearer, more detailed and specific" (p. 116). Comparing heaven to earth, he writes: "This is why heaven is not escapist: . . . we are already there, just as the fetus in the womb is already in the world. . . . We are not yet born from the world-womb, but we are already part of the heavenly body" (p. 174).

Lamont, Corliss. *The Illusion of Immortality.* Fifth edition. New York: Continuum Press, 1990 (first published 1965). This is a classic attack upon belief in a future life by a humanist. Lamont challenges the notion that death is an evil. "On the contrary," he argues, "death is an altogether natural thing and has played a useful and necessary role in the long course of biological evolution. . . . [It has] rendered possible the upward surge of organic species" (p. 269).

Lewis, C. S. *The Weight of Glory.* New York: Macmillan, 1949. No literary figure of the twentieth century has supported an orthodox Christian view of heaven more creatively than this late British author. Lewis perceives in people a lifelong nostalgia for eternal life. "At present," he writes, "we are on the outside of the world, the wrong side of the door. We discern the freshness and purity of morning, but they do not make us fresh and pure. We cannot mingle with the splendours we see. But all the leaves of the New Testament are rustling with the rumour that it will not always be so. Some day, God willing, we shall get *in*" (p. 113). Insights into eternal life appear within many of his books, including his Narnia series for children. In a remarkable fantasy, *The Great Divorce* (Macmillan, 1946), Lewis portrays a hell sustained by inhabitants, the "ghostly people," who are dissatisfied with heaven, which they visit by bus but refuse to stay in, even though entreated by the "solid people." Heaven's overwhelming reality terrifies them, and they can't accept God's grace. They prefer a diminishing realm in which they can retain their own selfish character even if they must keep moving about in the endless gray city to avoid folks they can't stand as neighbors. In this tale Lewis is sharply critical of theologians who deny the resurrection and have drifted into apostasy, becoming trapped in intellectual pride. Although the good "beats upon them as sound waves beat on the ears of the deaf, they cannot receive it. Their fists are clenched, their teeth are clenched, their eyes fast shut. First they will not, in the end they cannot, open their hands for gifts or their mouths for food, or open their eyes to see" (p. 127).

Luther, Martin. *Table Talk.* Translated by William Hazlitt. London: George Bell, 1884. About the new heaven and new earth Luther writes, "It will be no arid waste, but a beautiful new earth, where all the just will dwell together. There will be no carnivorous beasts, or venomous creatures, for all such, like ourselves, will be relieved from the curse of sin, and will be to us as friendly as they were to Adam in Paradise. There will be little dogs, with golden hair, shining like precious stones. The foliage of the trees, and the verdure of the grass, will have the brilliance of emeralds; and we ourselves, delivered from our mundane subjection to gross appetites and necessities, shall have the same form as here, but infinitely more perfect. Our eyes will be radiant as the purest silver, and we shall be exempt from all sickness and tribulation. We shall behold the glorious Creator face to face; and then, what ineffable satisfaction will it be to find our relations and friends among the just" (p. 332).

————. *Works,* vol. 28. St. Louis, MO: Concordia, 1973. Commenting on 1 Corinthians 15, this Reformation leader writes, "For He who is able to raise all the dead with one word will surely also know how to bestow a form and an essence that will serve and be appropriate to the heavenly, eternal life" (p. 175).

McDonnell, Colleen, and Bernhard Lang. *History of Heaven.* New Haven, CT: Yale, 1988. A useful compilation of historic views. In each era hopes of heaven offer a key to culture. In the medieval era the focus of the afterlife was upon contemplation. A romantic, anthropocentric view with a strong emphasis upon physical love characterized the nineteenth century. In the mid–twentieth century, under the influence of scientism, a symbolist view predominated as theologians sought to separate a religious meaning of heaven from a literal, scientific one. This approach went in two directions: liberal theologians transferred heaven to earth, while neo-orthodox scholars—"theocratic minimalists"—lodged heaven in the mind of God.

Migliore, Daniel L. *Faith Seeking Understanding.* Grand Rapids, MI: Eerdmans, 1991. This theologian links eschatology and ethics, with eternity offering boundaries and meaning to morality. In an appendix he constructs a dialogue about the resurrection between important twentieth-century thinkers Karl Barth, Rudolf Bultmann, Wolfhart Pannenberg, and Jürgen Moltmann (see below). Migliore honors Pannenberg for insisting that one must not split apart revelation and reason, faith and history, but must acknowledge that the resurrection is central to Christianity and that it occurs in reality.

Moltmann, Jürgen. *The Coming of God: Christian Eschatology.* Translated by Margaret Kohl. Minneapolis, MN: Fortress Press, 1996. A German theologian critiques views about eternity by Christian and Jewish thinkers, giving in-depth treatment to issues of eschatology, the meaning of God's kingdom, and the puzzling interface of space/time and eternity. This is one of the most thorough and perceptive modern treatments of eschatology. For Moltmann, Easter signals not just resurrection of the dead but the transfiguration of the whole cosmos. God's glory, hitherto veiled for the sake of creation, will in the new creation enhance time and space.

The Nag Hammadi Library. Third edition. Translated by James M. Robinson. San Francisco: HarperSanFrancisco, 1978. These ancient writings reflect a Gnostic point of view. "The Treatise on the Resurrection" describes eternity thus: "We are drawn to heaven by him [the Savior] like beams by the sun, not being restrained by anything. This is the spiritual resurrection which swallows up the psychic in the same way as the fleshly" (p. 55).

Neville, Robert Cummings. *Eternity and Time's Flow.* New York: State Univ. of New York Press, 1993. The author interprets the resurrection life as entering into God's plans. To overcome "the death of fragmentation and absurdity is to recover the sense of the divine mother who embraces all our parts and sets us on a path to make what true meaning we can" within our neighborhood and world, to let God's glory flow in the created world (p. 231).

Niemöller, Martin. *Dachau Sermons*. Translated by Robert H. Pfeiffer. New York: Harper & Brothers, 1946. This book contains poignant wartime reflections about the implications of Easter.

Oden, Thomas. *Life in the Spirit.* Vol. 3 of *Systematic Theology.* New York: HarperCollins, 1992. The author has compiled citations from Christian thinkers throughout the centuries and added commentary to each. Oden represents a growing centrist movement within Christianity. In an age addicted to accenting the peripheral in biblical interpretation, this biblical scholar reaffirms what has been and remains central to Christian belief. This particular volume concludes with an extensive treatment of "The End of Human History" and "The Communion of the Saints, Life Everlasting." These tenth and eleventh chapters provide a wealth of material concerning standard eschatological topics such as the second coming, the judgment, hell, and heaven. Oden exegetes germane biblical passages about the human condition in the afterlife and details historic interpretations of those passages. Following Hugh of St. Victor and Thomas Aquinas, Oden states this about the risen, glorified body: "[T]hat the risen body is spiritual does not imply that it has become so etherealized as to no longer be a body. It will be distinguishable from what it now is, yet still remain a body with the power of movement, yet without the digestive-reproductive function of the animal economy" (p. 405). "Though above reason," writes Oden, "resurrection is not contrary to reason, any more than is creation contrary to reason. Resurrection is simply a new creation. . . . If one can believe that the world has been created and exists in all its complexity, one can believe that the resurrection can occur in all its complexity" (p. 407).

Pache, René. *The Future Life*. Translated by Helen I. Needham. Chicago, IL: Moody, 1962. A strong affirmation by a French Bible scholar concerning traditional Christian teaching, with extensive biblical exegesis. The author envisions an earth partially renewed during the millennium, then destroyed completely to remove all stains of satanic revolt, and finally replaced by a new creation even more beautiful than the first one, and without sin.

Polkinghorne, John. *Belief in God in an Age of Science*. New Haven, CT: Yale Univ. Press, 1998. A well-reasoned plea for the complementary roles of religion and science by a British theologian/physicist. Polking-horne is critical of some recent efforts to subordinate the former to the latter—for example, "process theology," which he indicts for placing God "too much at the margins of the world" (p. 56).

————. *Faith in the Living God.* Philadelphia, PA: Westminster, 2001. Polkinghorne engages in a dialogue with Michael Welker, a professor at Heidelberg University (and, like Polkinghorne, a fervent Christian believer), on issues relating to God as Creator and Redeemer.

————. *Science and Theology.* Minneapolis, MN: SPCK/Fortress 1998. Polkinghorne sketches the historical interaction between science and theology and presents a scientific picture of the world in relationship with humanity and God. He summarizes the account of the resurrection of Jesus and weighs the evidence. To him "it makes sense," for it signifies that God did not abandon the one he sent, that Jesus' life was not a failure, and that "Jesus anticipates within history a destiny that awaits all other human beings beyond history" (p. 106).

————. *The God of Hope and the End of the World.* New Haven, CT: Yale Univ. Press, 2002. A useful summary of scientific, biblical, and theological reasons why physical resurrection is credible.

Quaker Religious Thought, vol. 29.4, no. 94, Feb. 2000. This issue includes editor Paul Anderson's article "On Jesus: Quests for Historicity, and the History of the Recent Quests," and an extensive bibliography of recent studies of the historical Jesus. Anderson recalls the classic words of an earlier questing scholar, Albert Schweitzer, who left theological studies to serve as a medical doctor in Africa: "He comes to us as One unknown. . . . He speaks to us the same word, 'Follow thou me!'" Anderson concludes that the "catalyzing intersection of connecting the Jesus of history with the Christ of faith is the changed and changing lives of those seeking to attend, discern, and heed the present leadings of the risen Christ for today" (p. 31). A later issue—vol. 30.4, no. 98—contains responses to this presentation by several scholars, including Marcus Borg, who defends the "Jesus Seminar" quest, and Gary Kinkel, who indicts it. Professor Kinkel avers that "by limiting 'the real Jesus' to naturalistic canons of modernism, his authority is reduced to relativity" (p. 40). Professor Anderson offers a response, noting that this debate continues a dialogue which historically has resulted in affirming both the humanity and the deity of Jesus Christ. He hopes that will be the result of this round.

Roberts, Arthur O. *Messengers of God: The Sensuous Side of Spirituality.* Newberg, OR: Barclay Press, 1996. Starting from the biblical premise that the body is the temple of the Holy Spirit, and from a well-known phrase from Augustine that refers to the senses as "messengers of God," the author delineates practical discipleship for each of the senses. The book includes physiological descriptions, by a granddaughter, Robin Roberts, of what occurs physiologically in our God-given neuroreceptors. Believing that contemporary sensory overload is especially damaging to children, the author meets sensate culture on its own grounds and reclaims it for religious faith. "Have confidence in the senses!" he concludes. "Care for them as visiting angels. They are God's messengers of hope. Spiritual reality drums its song bodily with each heartbeat. The eye, the ear, the nose, the palate, the hand—each throbs with the pulse of the Holy Spirit" (p. 188).

———. *Prayers at Twilight.* Newberg, OR: Barclay Press, 2003. This poetry expresses struggles of ordinary people to envision a meaningful afterlife and to express their hopes for heaven. A few of these poems appear in *Exploring Heaven.*

Schep, J. A. *The Nature of the Resurrection Body.* Grand Rapids, MI: Eerdmans, 1964. This Australian Bible scholar holds the view that the resurrection body will be a body of flesh. He analyzes the various ways in which the word *flesh* is used in the Bible—sometimes as a synonym for evil (e.g., "heart of stone" or "sinful flesh") and at other times as a synonym for weakness and finiteness. He shows that the physical body is understood as a good creation, honored of God and redeemed through Christ. Schep exegetes Paul's use of the term *flesh* to show that it connotes corrupt human nature, not a nonembodied state of existence. Schep rejects any view that deifies humanity in the afterlife. "Whatever resurrection-body man may have in eternity," he writes, "he will always remain finite . . . for he can never cease to be a *creature* in both body and soul" (p. 21).

Smith, Huston. "Intimations of Immortality," Ingersoll Lecture for 2001–2002, *Harvard Divinity School Bulletin,* vol. 30, no. 3, Winter 2001–2002. This eminent authority on world religions offers a sequel to Carol Zaleski's provocative lecture of the previous year (see below). Smith proposes three case studies to support cultural intimations of immortality. He concludes that "religion invariably wagers on immortality."

————. *Why Religion Matters: The Fate of the Human Spirit in an Age of Disbelief.* San Francisco: HarperSanFrancisco, 2001. In this publication the renowned author of *The World's Religions* offers a penetrating analysis of the culture of our time. He finds both modernity and postmodernism too narrow. He opts rather to support a traditional worldview in which religions constitute the primary humanizing force for humanity. Smith is committed to religion that transcends phoniness and "makes people real." "The whole object of religion," he asserts, "is to enable people to come as close as possible to God's infinite reality. That should be easy, because God is so real that we should respond like iron filings to his magnetic pull" (p. 231, all citations). It's the fact that human beings are so *unreal* that makes the task hard.

Smith, Wilbur M. *The Biblical Doctrine of Heaven.* Chicago: Moody Press, 1968. This book provides expositions about biblical passages dealing with heaven. Smith favors the picture of heaven as "the abode of God," which picture he finds reinforced by such biblical terms as *tabernacle, temple,* and *sanctuary.* These terms convey themes of holiness and intimate relationships.

Teilhard de Chardin, Pierre. *The Divine Milieu.* New York: Harper & Row, 1960. This Jesuit anthropologist affirms the "cosmic Christ," whom he identifies in essays and letters, against possible misunderstanding, as Jesus Christ of Nazareth, the crucified and risen One. In his earlier *Phenomenon of Man,* he describes the exponential swarming of intelligence, calling it the leading edge of evolution, which in his more explicit religious writings he identifies forthrightly as the material milieu for the recreating and redeeming work of Christ.

Tertullian. *On the Resurrection of the Flesh.* Vol. 3 of *Ante-Nicene Christian Fathers.* Grand Rapids, MI: Christian Classics Ethereal Library (Internet version), 2002. This second-century treatise remains one of the fullest treatments of heaven in Christian literature. A lawyer from Carthage, North Africa, converted in middle life, Tertullian became a brilliant apologist for the Christian faith. At great length he affirmed the resurrection of the body and not just the soul. In today's terms, he held a "holistic" view of the human person. He also rejected any deification of man in the afterlife (chap. 2). "God forbid," Tertullian insisted, "that He should abandon to everlasting destruction the labour of His own hands, the care of His own thoughts, the receptacle of His own Spirit, the queen of His creation, the inheritor of His own liberality, the priestess of His religion, the champion of His testimony, the sister of His Christ! We know by experience the goodness of God; from His Christ we learn that He is the only God, and the very good" (chap. 9). Tertullian rejected the notion that bodily resurrection must be understood figuratively. He wrote: "If things which pertain to the body are figurative, why are not those which pertain to the soul figurative also? Since, however, things which belong to the soul have nothing allegorical in them, neither therefore have those which belong to the body. For man is as much body as he is soul; so that it is impossible for one of these natures to admit a figurative sense, and the other to exclude it" (chap. 32).

Thielicke, Helmut. *Death and Life.* Philadelphia, PA: Fortress, 1970 (from the 1946 edition translated by Edward H. Schroeder). This German theologian, writing in wartime, pondered the meaning of death: "My death," he wrote, "is transfigured into the death of Jesus Christ. It now carries the signature of the second Adam and no longer that of the first. . . . I surrender to the new destiny that awaits me in Christ. . . . We stand in the realm of the Resurrected One's power. . . . [W]here he is I will be" (p. 200).

Vanauken, Sheldon. *A Severe Mercy.* San Francisco: HarperSan-Francisco, 1980. This autobiographical love story details how an irreligious young couple fell in love and were brought to a vital Christian faith and a heightened understanding of love through the writings of and conversation with C. S. Lewis. The untimely death of the young wife, Jean ("Davy"), leads to thoughtful affirmations of eternal life.

Walls, Jerry L. *Heaven: The Logic of Eternal Joy.* New York: Oxford Univ. Press, 2002. This is a closely reasoned apologetic for Christian doctrines concerning heaven. Like me, Walls finds the time ripe for re-affirming these doctrines, and similarly draws upon scientists as well as theologians to support his view. Walls begins his apologetic task philo-sophically, by refuting the naturalistic assumptions of the empiricist philosopher so seminal for the modern era, David Hume, and then links doctrines of heaven logically with the goodness of God. Walls argues persuasively that human happiness and morality are grounded upon a belief in heaven. "To believe in God is to believe happiness is stronger than boredom. It is to believe that our transient delights in this life are invitations to enter eternal happiness and that the author of the invita-tions is fully worthy of our trust" (p. 197).

―――. *Hell: The Logic of Damnation.* Notre Dame, IN: Notre Dame Univ. Press, 1992. This book deals with the implications of liber-tarian freedom, the choosing of irresponsible being. God's optimal grace, according to Walls, justifies allowing such significant choice.

―――. "Purgatory for Everyone." *First Things,* Apr. 2002. This arti-cle is drawn from Walls's book *Heaven* (see above). This Wesleyan scholar at Asbury Seminary believes a case can be made for purgatory for everyone, not as punishment but as a time for completing the process of sanctification. Walls asserts that a theology of holiness makes this condi-tion more logical than positing temporary punishment, as in Roman Catholic tradition, or positing instantaneous completion of sanctifica-tion "at the article of death," as in Reformed theology.

Whatever Happened to the Soul? Scientific and Theological Portraits. Edited by Warren S. Brown, Nancey Murphy, and H. Newton Malony. A volume in a series of *Theology and the Sciences.* Minneapolis, MN: Augsburg/Fortress, 1998. The series is another example of the continuing creative interface between science and religion, featuring some of the world's most astute scholars in both fields. In this volume the contributors reject the old dualism (or any new dualism) of body and spirit. They consider that the term *soul* means the God-given principle of human life. In a concluding chapter editor Warren Brown writes: "In order for the portrait of human nature suggested in these essays to be credible we need to have not only a nonreductive science of human nature, but a physicalist theology." This position about human nature "accepts and profits from both scientific and theological accounts of humankind since the supervenience of higher-level explanations on lower-level explanations is allowed." Most important, Brown notes, "a nonreductive physicalist point of view forces one to attempt to reconcile theological and scientific accounts" (pp. 227–228).

Whittier, John Greenleaf. *The Poetry of John Greenleaf Whittier.* Edited by William Jolliff. Richmond, IN: Friends United Press, 2000. Among American poets, Whittier uniquely blends a passionate concern for social righteousness with a passionate hope for heaven. The well-loved poem "At Last" includes these lines:

> *Suffice it if—my good and ill unreckoned,*
> *And both forgiven through Thy abounding grace—*
> *I find myself by hands familiar beckoned*
> *Unto my fitting place.*
> *Some humble door among Thy many mansions,*
> *Some sheltering shade where sin and striving cease,*
> *And flows forever through heaven's green expansions*
> *The river of Thy peace.*
> *There, from the music round about me stealing,*
> *I fain would learn the new and holy song,*
> *And find at last, beneath Thy trees of healing,*
> *The life for which I long.*

Willard, Dallas. *The Divine Conspiracy.* San Francisco: HarperSanFrancisco, 1998. Chap. 10, "The Restoration of All Things," affirms the continuity of material life, a boon to people frustrated by not having achieved in this life what they wanted or were capable of. Willard affirms the goodness of creation and its continuity in heaven.

Williams, H. A. *True Resurrection*. New York: Holt, Rinehart, Winston, 1972. The author warns against applying to the future life the logic of desire rather than the logic of hope. Regarding the tension between continuity and discontinuity, he tilts toward the latter. Too much speculation about continuities can make heaven look ridiculous, he says; but the logic of hope allows us to transcend the limits of our perceptions.

Wills-Brandon, Carla. *One Last Hug Before I Go*. Health Communications, 2000. This therapist and mathematics teacher maintains an Internet website, carla.wills.brandon.net, on which are narrated near-death experiences. Her writings include some of these stories. As a logician Wills-Brandon is impressed by glimpses of the hereafter that don't fit preconceptions—e.g., a child who wonders why the angels she saw had no wings.

Yancey, Philip. *The Jesus I Never Knew*. Grand Rapids, MI: Zondervan, 1995. One of the finest current studies of Jesus available. Yancey's analysis of the biblical texts about Jesus' resurrection shows that it was the authorities who demonstrated collusion by trying to discount the empty tomb. He effectively refutes the charge that the followers of Jesus conspired to make up the resurrection accounts.

Zaleski, Carol. "In Defense of Immortality," Ingersoll Lecture for 2000, *Harvard Divinity School Bulletin*, vol. 29, no. 2. The author, a professor of religion and literature at Smith College, analyzes the recent reluctance of the academic community to believe in an afterlife, critiques various views of immortality, and opts for "Omega immortality," which she considers basic to Jewish and Christian eschatologies and compatible with humanity created in God's image and destined for eternity. She urges a return to awe before the Almighty, a willingness to replace self-assertion with humility, and an acknowledgment that with God all things are possible.

———. *The Life of the World to Come*. New York: Oxford Univ. Press, 1996. In this work Zaleski focuses upon what near-death experiences signify: not objective evidence, but an underscoring of Christian hope. She envisions the afterlife as a real world in which species and persons are preserved.

———, with Phillip Zaleski. *The Book of Heaven: An Anthology.* New York: Oxford Univ. Press, 2000. This is a helpful summary of historic hopes and visions for the afterlife.

NOTES

The abbreviation *CWS*, which appears in many notes, refers to *Classics of Western Spirituality*, an ongoing series published in New York by Paulist Press. Publication dates for specific volumes are given in the notes.

The abbreviation *HDRVD* refers to *How Different Religions View Death and the Afterlife*, 2nd ed., ed. C. J. Johnson and M. G. McGee (Philadelphia, PA: Charles Press, 1998).

The abbreviation *LCC* refers to *Library of Christian Classics*, a series published in Philadelphia by Westminster Press. Publication dates for specific volumes are given in the notes.

CHAPTER ONE

1. Arthur O. Roberts, *Prayers at Twilight* (Newberg, OR: Barclay Press, 2003).
2. Paul K. Jewett, *God, Creation, and Revelation* (Grand Rapids: Eerdmans, 1991), pp. 467ff.
3. Huston Smith, *Why Religion Matters: The Fate of the Human Spirit in an Age of Disbelief* (San Francisco: HarperSanFrancisco, 2001), p. 157. Publication information for the other books noted appears in the Annotated Bibliography.
4. A colleague at George Fox University, Dwight Kimberly, an Oregon teacher of the year, was honored recently by Templeton for a program helping elementary instructors teach science. An example of Templeton support for international scholarly dialogue on issues of science and religion is a 2003 conference at the University of Notre Dame titled "God and Physical Cosmology," which involved leading philosophers, theologians, and cosmologists from the United States, Great Britain, and Russia.

CHAPTER TWO

1. *Native Mesoamerican Spirituality,* in *CWS* (New York: Paulist Press, 1981), p. 183; from the Nahuatl language.
2. John 14:3.
3. Corliss Lamont, *The Illusion of Immortality,* 5th ed. (New York: Continuum Press, 1990; first published, 1965), p. 277.
4. Smith, *Why Religion Matters,* p. 20 and passim. Smith faults Sagan for treating an unargued assumption as fact. He also criticizes both modernity and postmodernity as inadequate to account for reality—the first for assuming that a materialistic worldview could account for everything, including mind and spirit, the second for assuming that there *is* no worldview, no "meganarrative," but only local stories, all of which should be tolerated (though postmodernity offers no reasons why). Smith opts for the traditional metaphysic, which makes room for immaterial as well as material reality.
5. *Selected Poems of Horace,* ed. George F. Whicher (New York: Walter J. Black, The Classics Club, 1947), p. 8.
6. Roberts, *Prayers at Twilight* (Newberg, OR: Barclay Press, 2003).
7. Sharafuddin Maneri, *The Hundred Letters,* in *CWS* (New York: Paulist Press, 1980). Letter 100 describes how a person entering paradise bathes in one of two streams of destiny, is cleansed, and is given the damsel destined for him, found by one of his slaves. He then is united with his wives and goes to a mansion built of emeralds and rubies and other gems. The person entering heaven will notice that there's a rank there—lower windows, higher windows. The highest reality is a vision of God, which is beyond good deeds. Some persons experience this once a month or once a week; others, continuously. This is beyond merit. "No, it is due, purely and simply, to the Grace of God" (p. 423).
8. Frederick Buechner, *Wishful Thinking: A Seeker's ABC,* rev. ed. (San Francisco: HarperSanFrancisco, 1993), pp. 51–52.
9. *Meister Eckhart, Treatises,* in *CWS* (New York: Paulist Press, 1981), p. 216.
10. Charles Hartshorne, *The Logic of Perfection,* cited in Jürgen Moltmann, *The Coming of God: Christian Eschatology* (Minneapolis, MN: Fortress, 1996), pp. 338–339.
11. Huston Smith considers the "process theology" of Hartshorne to have been but another form of mid-twentieth-century naturalistic theism. He writes, in *Why Religion Matters:* "Its God is not an exception to principles that order this world, but their chief exemplar. God is not outside time as its Creator, but within it" (p. 74).

12. "Prospect of Heaven Makes Death Easier," *The Poets' Corner* (www.poets'-corner.org).

13. "Holy Sonnets," no. 6, *John Donne,* in *CWS* (New York: Paulist Press, 1990), p. 80.

CHAPTER THREE

1. Bonaventure, *The Tree of Life,* in *CWS* (New York: Paulist Press, 1978), p. 173.

2. Francois Fénelon, *Christian Perfection* (New York: Harper & Brothers, 1947), no. 27, p. 104.

3. Abdu'l Baha, *Some Answered Questions,* cited in *How Different Religions View Death and the Afterlife,* 2nd ed., ed. C. J. Johnson and M. G. McGee (Philadelphia, PA: Charles Press, 1998), pp. 28–29.

4. Freely cited from a succinct summary of the topic in the *Oxford Dictionary of the Christian Church,* 3rd ed., ed. E. A. Livingstone (New York: Oxford Univ. Press, 1997), p. 564.

5. I'm indebted to Wendell Barnett for this phrasing about sparrows. See his devotional for Apr. 11, 2002, in *Fruit of the Vine* (Newberg, OR: Barclay Press, 2002).

6. Ian G. Barbour, *Religion and Science: Historical and Contemporary Issues* (San Francisco: HarperSanFrancisco, 1997), p. 272.

7. Summaries of Jewish and Islamic views appear in *HDRVD;* the Jewish view cited is from p. 151.

8. Phil Smith, letter to the author, Aug. 22, 2002. Smith is a George Fox University professor of philosophy.

9. Jerry L. Walls, *Hell: The Logic of Damnation* (Notre Dame, IN: Notre Dame Univ. Press, 1992), p. 155.

10. *HDRVD,* p. 140. Islamic thought contrasts heaven and hell with symbols of garden and fire.

11. "The Believer," *The Koran,* 4.76 (electronic version from http://etext.virginia.edu/).

12. Stephen T. Davis, *Risen Indeed: Making Sense of the Resurrection* (Grand Rapids, MI: Eerdmans, 1993), p. 156.

13. C. S. Lewis, *The Great Divorce* (New York: Macmillan, 1946), esp. p. 23. Lewis contrasts the ghostly nature of those in hell with the "solid people" in heaven, and his tale includes conversations in which heavenly persons try to convince the visitors to accept God's grace and remain; but none do, preferring rather to nurse their grievances and justify themselves.

14. Clark Pinnock's position is noted in *Four Views of Hell,* ed. William Crockett (Grand Rapids, MI: Zondervan, 1992).

15. Peter Kreeft, *Heaven: The Heart's Deepest Longing* (San Francisco, CA: Ignatius Press, 1989), p. 174.

16. *HDRVD,* p. 142.

17. Thomas Aquinas, *Summa Theologica,* 2nd rev. ed., 1920. Literally translated by Fathers of the English Dominican Province (online edition copyright © 2000 by Kevin Knight), Appendix II, citing Augustine, *De Civ Dei* i.8. The doctrine claims that a New Testament basis can be found in Paul's teaching (1 Cor. 3:10–15) about what endures (because founded on Christ) and what does not, comparing gold and silver with wood and straw, tested in the fire. Some scholars interpret the text otherwise, to refer to the church rather than to individuals.

18. "Purgatory," *Oxford Dictionary of the Christian Church,* 3rd ed., ed. E. A. Livingstone (New York: Oxford Univ. Press, 1997). The *Catholic Encyclopedia* also succinctly summarizes Roman Catholic views about purgatory. (There have been many editions of the Catholic Encyclopedia over the past century. It is available on the Internet at www.newadvent.org.cathen, edited by Kevin Knight, 2002.)

19. John Calvin, *Institutes of the Christian Religion,* from book 3, "Meditation on the Future Life" (Philadelphia, PA: Westminster Press, 1955), chap. 9.5, p. 716.

20. See *Barclay's Apology in Modern English,* ed. Dean Freiday (Newberg, OR: Barclay Press, 1967), propositions 8 and 9; citation from p. 156.

21. See his "Christian Perfection," here cited from *John and Charles Wesley,* in *CWS* (New York: Paulist Press, 1991), especially pp. 322ff.

22. *HDRVD,* p. 122.

23. *HDRVD,* p. 141.

24. Jerry L. Walls, "Purgatory for Everyone," *First Things,* Apr. 2002. The article is drawn from his book *Heaven: The Logic of Eternal Joy* (New York: Oxford Univ. Press, 2002).

CHAPTER FOUR

1. Owen Gingerich, *Evidence of Purpose,* ed. John Marks Templeton (New York: Continuum, 1994), p. 32. Harvard astronomer Gingerich concludes his essay on evidence of purpose with the words quoted here.

2. Joseph F. Girzone, *Joshua and the Children* (New York: Macmillan, 1989), pp. 58–59. (These are the words of Joshua, the Jesus figure, talking to the Irish children.)

3. Angela of Foligno, *Complete Works,* in *CWS* (New York: Paulist Press, 1993), see pp. 309–310.

4. Following eighteenth-century philosopher Immanuel Kant, modern philosophers and theologians argued that pure reason could as easily negate as affirm divine causality. For some, proving the existence of God on the basis of what Kant called "practical reason" offered a viable alternative to the medieval proofs. For others, following Kierkegaard, even moral purpose lacked logical certainty; an Abrahamic leap of faith was required and sufficed. Recently, arguments from design and purpose have found renewed support, based not upon pure or practical reason but upon probability linked with faith in God.

5. David Grindspoon, writing in *Astronomy,* May 2000, says in an article titled "SETI and the Star Wars" that "a reductionist, universalist, scientific philosophy is an unspoken assumption of SETI" (Search for Extraterrestrial Intelligence). He's very unhappy with postmodernists who would dismiss scientific knowledge as culturally derived. Although there's a cultural side, science is basically discovery and not invention. It's not just one text—one story—among many. "Most anyone who has experienced scientific discovery has a strong conviction that the universe is trying to tell us something." He thinks discovery of other intelligence would verify universals. (This search is an example of socially constructed science and embodies a leap of faith.) He believes SETI would enable us to recognize universals, because the evidence wouldn't reflect our biases or hypotheses. It would be testable. "SETI is a test of our faith in science, a test of the nature of scientific truth." He concludes: "Are scientific laws and discoveries constructs of the human mind or are they revelations of aspects of nature that exist completely independently of us? One sure fire way to find out would be to borrow a physics textbook from the nearest ET and compare notes."

6. One can approach the evidence for purposeful intelligence another way. Philosophy consists of two basic issues (and extensive commentaries on them), and science adds a third: (1) the relationship between the one and the many, (2) the relationship between permanence and change, and (3) a tension between continuity and discontinuity. Intelligent purpose offers coherence to these tensions: many parts are connected; what is temporal melds with what is eternal. New orders of reality arise unpredictably but coherently. If one accepts the "word of nature" as a part of divine revelation, then one can read certain natural signs as affirming divine intelligence. Among these signs are: the conservation of energy, the arrow of time, the complexity of things, order and design, and an exponential and relatively rapid spread of intelligence.

7. John Polkinghorne, *Science and Theology* (Minneapolis, MN: SPCK/ Fortress 1998), pp. 36–37. Not all scientists, of course, consider that purposive intelligence requires a divine source. See, for example, Mihaly Csikszentmihalyi, in *The Evolving Self*, noted in the Annotated Bibliography.

8. John Eccles, *Evidence of Purpose: Scientists Discover the Creator*, edited by John Marks Templeton (New York: Continuum, 1994), p. 132. Much credit for bringing scholars of the word of nature together with scholars of the word of Scripture goes to Sir John Templeton, businessman and Christian philanthropist. In his introduction Templeton concurs with the person who said that "coincidence is God's way of remaining anonymous" (p. 16).

9. *Native Mesoamerican Spirituality*, in *CWS* (New York: Paulist Press, 1980), pp. 176ff.

10. *Native Mesoamerican Spirituality*, in *CWS*, citing *Collection of Mexican Songs*, folio v, pp. 186–187.

11. Sheldon and Jean Vanauken, *A Severe Mercy* (San Francisco: HarperSan-Francisco, 1980), pp. 222–223.

12. Gary R. Habermas and J. P. Moreland, *Beyond Death: Exploring the Evidence for Immortality* (Wheaton, IL: Crossway Books, 1998).

13. From Carla Wills-Brandon's Web site: http://carla.wills.brandon.net.

14. Habermas and Moreland, in *Beyond Death* (p. 167), tell of experiments by a leading neurosurgeon, Wilder Penfield, whose clinical tests contradicted his earlier hypothesis that "neuronal action within the brain must account for all the mind does," cited from *The Mystery of the Mind* (Princeton: Princeton Univ. Press, 1975), pp. 76–77. Huston Smith agrees.

15. Philip Yancey's analysis of the biblical texts, in *The Jesus I Never Knew* (Grand Rapids, MI: Zondervan, 1995), shows that it wasn't believers who demonstrated collusion in the resurrection stories, but the authorities who tried to explain the empty tomb. The initial unbelief of Jesus' followers and their varying testimony indicates bewilderment, yes—but certainly not calculated collusion.

16. Carol Zaleski, "In Defense of Immortality," *Harvard Divinity School Bulletin*, vol. 29, no. 2 (2000), pp. 12, 16, and 17.

17. Huston Smith, "Intimations of Immortality," *Harvard Divinity School Bulletin*, vol. 30, no. 3 (2001–2002), p. 15. Smith claims that neurotheology is just the "latest form of reductionism" and that mind cannot ever be reduced to brain.

18. Paul Anderson, "On Jesus: Quests for Historicity, and the History of the Recent Quests," *Quaker Religious Thought*, vol. 29.4, no. 94 (Feb. 2000), pp. 30–31.

19. Such a scenario is central in a theologically astute mystery novel by P. D. James, *Death in Holy Orders* (New York: Ballantine Books, 2001). The setting is a small and failing Anglican seminary, fittingly named St. Anselm, whose old buildings contain valuable religious art, including, in a secure vault, an ancient and coveted papyrus purporting to detail finding the bones of Jesus. Was the papyrus authentic, or fake? Old Father Martin concludes that its release for testing would only fuel inconclusive and acrimonious argument. When detective Dalgliesh asks whether it would make a difference to his faith if it were authentic, Martin replies, "My son, for one who every hour of his life has the assurance of the living presence of Christ, why should I worry about what happened to earthly bones?" (p. 429).

20. For a thorough discussion of recent critiques of Jesus' resurrection, see Habermas and Moreland, *Beyond Death*. A brief synopsis of the main issues, by Loren King and Paul Anderson, appears in *Quaker Religious Thought*, vols. 27-2 and 27-4, nos. 84 and 85 (1995).

21. Paul Copan and Ronald K. Tacelli, eds., *Jesus' Resurrection: Fact or Fiction?* (Downers Grove, IL: InterVarsity Press, 2000), p. 161.

22. Lüdemann, *Jesus' Resurrection*, p. 206.

23. Lüdemann, *Jesus' Resurrection*, p. 85.

24. Tertullian, *On the Resurrection of the Flesh*, in *Ante-Nicene Christian Fathers* (Grand Rapids, MI: The Christian Classics Ethereal Library, Internet version), chap. 2, p. 11.

25. Athenagoras, "A Plea Regarding Christians," in *Early Christian Fathers*, vol. 1 of *Library of Christian Classics (LCC)* (Philadelphia: Westminster, 1953), p. 311. His plea was addressed to emperors Marcus Aurelius and Commodius, "and—what is most important—philosophers."

26. Justin Martyr, "Fragments of the Lost Work of Justin on the Resurrection," trans. M. Dods, in *Ante-Nicene Christian Fathers*, vol. 1 (Grand Rapids, MI: The Christian Classics Ethereal Library, Internet version), chap. 10, p. 298.

27. Jürgen Moltmann, *The Coming of God: Christian Eschatology*, trans. Margaret Kohl (Minneapolis: Fortress Press, 1996), p. 75.

28. John Polkinghorne, *Science and Theology* (Minneapolis, MN: SPCK/Fortress 1998), p. 107.

29. Robert Jastrow, *God and the Astronomers* (New York: Warner Books, 1984), pp. 124–125, cited by Arthur Peacocke in "Science and the Creator," *Evidence of Purpose*, ed. John Marks Templeton (New York: Continuum, 1994), p. 92. Professor Diogenes Allen, Princeton theologian, rightly notes, however, that "God is the *source* of all things and that science deals only with the transformation and relations between *existing* things" (p. 178).

Hence neither theologian nor scientist can reach to creation's beginning, which remains ever within the mystery of God's creative, sustaining activity. See Allen's *Christian Belief in a Postmodern World: The Full Wealth of Conviction* (Louisville, KY: Westminster/John Knox Press, 1989).

30. Michael Welker, "Resurrection and Eternal Life," in *The End of the World and the Ends of God,* ed. John Polkinghorne and Michael Welker (Harrisburg, PA: Trinity Press International, 2000), p. 283. In this essay Welker also lists alternative views about what happened to Jesus and offers a critique of them.

31. Welker, "Resurrection and Eternal Life," p. 288.

32. John Greenleaf Whittier, from "My Psalm," *The Poetry of John Greenleaf Whittier,* ed. William Jolliff (Richmond, IN: Friends United Press, 2000), p. 240.

33. Martin Niemöller, *Dachau Sermons,* trans. Robert H. Pfeiffer (New York: Harper & Brothers, 1946), pp. 88, 95.

CHAPTER FIVE

1. C. S. Lewis, *The Weight of Glory* (New York: Macmillan, 1949), pp. 39–40.

2. Pearl Crist Hall, *Long Road to Freedom: One Person's Discovery of Death* (Richmond, IN: Friends United Press, 1978), p. 100.

3. Karl Barth, *Dogmatics of Creation,* vol. 3:3, "Doctrine of Creation" (Edinburgh: Clark, 1936–1969), p. 513.

4. The Angel Museum displays its artwork on a Web site: http://www.angel-museum.com.

5. Billy Graham, *Angels: God's Secret Agents* (New York: Doubleday, 1975).

6. Peter Kreeft, *Angels (and Demons)* (San Francisco: Ignatius Press, 1995), question 66.

7. Father Peter Gregory, "Online Prayers," http://www.transchurch.org/sguide/praybk.htm.

8. Vachel Lindsay's poem "General William Booth Enters into Heaven" has appeared in various collections, including the work from which this poem was taken, *The Congo and Other Poems* (Macmillan, 1915). I have used an early text in an Internet collection, *The Poets' Corner* (www.poets'-corner.org).

9. William R. Uhl, Sisualik, AK, letter to the author, May 15, 2002. The initial part of the spiritual journey of this Christian naturalist may be found in the chapter "Bob Uhl's Search for Eden," in Arthur O. Roberts, *Tomorrow Is Growing Old: Stories of the Quakers in Alaska* (Newberg, OR: Barclay Press,

1978). Uhl is a consultant on Arctic environmental and cultural issues for government agencies and writers of magazine articles. He became a Christian, as well as a keen observer of nature, through the influence of the Eskimo family into which he married.

10. Ian G. Barbour, *Religion and Science: Historical and Contemporary Issues*, rev. ed. (San Francisco: HarperSanFrancisco, 1997), p. 215.

CHAPTER SIX

1. Phil. 3:10–11.

2. Tertullian, *On the Resurrection of the Flesh*, in *Ante-Nicene Christian Fathers* (Grand Rapids, MI: The Christian Classics Ethereal Library, Internet version), chap. 9.

3. Thomas C. Oden, *Life in the Spirit*, vol. 3 of *Systematic Theology* (San Francisco: HarperSanFrancisco, 1992), p. 402.

4. I incorporate Augustine's phrase for the senses in the title of a book, *Messengers of God: The Sensuous Side of Spirituality* (Newberg, OR: Barclay Press, 1996), which deals with earthside disciplines appropriate to affirming one's body as the temple of the Holy Spirit.

5. Ian G. Barbour, *Religion and Science*, pp. 270–271.

6. J. A. Schep, *The Nature of the Resurrection Body* (Grand Rapids, MI: Eerdmans, 1964), p. 21.

7. Irenaeus of Lyons (ca. 170), *Against Heresies*, vol. 1 of *Early Christian Fathers*, in *LCC* (Philadelphia, PA: Westminster, 1953), p. 396.

8. D. Elton Trueblood, *Philosophy of Religion* (New York: Harper & Brothers, 1957), p. 295. Trueblood considered scientific and philosophical arguments for an afterlife inconclusive but religious argument fruitful. See "Evidence for Survival," pp. 296ff, esp. p. 303.

9. Ray S. Anderson, "On Being Human," in *Whatever Happened to the Soul? Scientific and Theological Portraits*, ed. Warren S. Brown, Nancey Murphy, and H. Newton Malony, in the series *Theology and the Sciences* (Minneapolis, MN: Augsburg/Fortress, 1998), p. 189.

10. Augustine, *Confessions and Enchiridion*, vol. 7 of *LCC*, trans. and ed. Albert C. Outler (Philadelphia, PA: Westminster, 1955), p. 392. This giant among early Christian thinkers deals concretely with the resurrection in chap. 23 of the *Enchiridion*. He bucked the tide of philosophical idealism to reinforce biblical doctrine about the dignity and worth of the material creation, insisting that humanity was clay before being invested with spirit.

11. Augustine, *Confessions and Enchiridion*, p. 390.

12. Arthur O. Roberts, *Prayers at Twilight* (Newberg, OR: Barclay Press, 2003).

13. Augustine, *Confessions and Enchiridion,* p. 403.

14. Johannes Wollebius, in *Reformed Dogmatics,* trans. and ed. John W. Beardslee III (New York: Oxford Univ. Press, 1965), p. 189.

15. Richard Baxter, *The Saints' Everlasting Rest,* abridged by Benjamin Fawcett (Kidderminster, UK: 1758), p. 64. Reprint New York: American Tract Society, n.d.

CHAPTER SEVEN

1. Sharafuddin Maneri, *The Hundred Letters,* in *CWS* (New York: Paulist Press, 1980), "Letter 27, Imitation of the Messenger."

2. Miroslav Volf, cited in *The End of the World and the Ends of God: Science and Theology on Eschatology,* ed. John Polkinghorne and Michael Welker (Harrisburg, PA: Trinity Press, 2000), p. 261.

3. Baxter, *The Saints' Everlasting Rest,* pp. 61, 68.

4. Garth L. Hallett, "The Tedium of Immortality," in *Faith and Philosophy,* vol. 18, no. 3 (July 2001), p. 288.

5. Emanuel Swedenborg, *The Universal Human and Soul-Body Interaction,* in *CWS* (New York: Paulist Press, 1984), p. 137.

6. H. A. Williams, *True Resurrection* (New York: Holt, Rinehart, Winston, 1972), p. 36.

7. John Calvin, *Institutes of the Christian Religion* (Philadelphia: Westminster, 1955 edition), xxv, 10, p. 1006.

8. John Gilmore, *Probing Heaven: Key Questions* (Grand Rapids, MI: Baker Book House, 1989 and 1993), p. 294.

9. Wilbur Smith, *The Biblical Doctrine of Heaven* (Chicago, IL: Moody Press, 1968), p. 190.

CHAPTER EIGHT

1. Arthur O. Roberts, *Prayers at Twilight* (Newberg, OR: Barclay Press, 2003).

2. Warren S. Brown, "Reconciling Scientific and Biblical Portraits of Human Nature," in *Whatever Happened to the Soul?* p. 227.

3. Miroslav Volf, cited in *The End of the World and the Ends of God,* p. 264.

4. Maneri, *The Hundred Letters,* "Letter 100," p. 422. But the same goes for securing a flying carpet or a fine stallion to ride, and such wishes are considered lower-level desires.

5. C. S. Lewis, cited from *The Problem of Pain* in *The Complete C. S. Lewis Signature Classics* (San Francisco: HarperSanFrancisco, 2002), p. 429.

6. As reported in a story in the *Washington Post* by Susan Schmidt, appearing in a Eugene, Oregon, newspaper, the *Register Guard* (Aug. 10, 2002).

7. Jacques Ellul, *The Meaning of the City* (Grand Rapids, MI: Eerdmans, 1970). Ellul asserts that although on earth God accommodates to human desires, in heaven God will render to humans "the setting he preferred" (pp. 176–177).

8. Richard Baxter, *The Saints' Everlasting Rest,* passim.

CHAPTER NINE

1. Dallas Willard, *The Divine Conspiracy* (San Francisco: HarperSanFrancisco, 1998), p. 378.

2. Brian Greene, *The Elegant Universe* (New York: Vintage Books, 1999), p. 387.

3. Ray C. Stedman, "The City of Glory," a sermon, Apr. 1990 (from Web site http://www.pbc.org/dp/stedman/bio.html).

4. Rom. 8:19–21.

5. See, for example, Greene, *The Elegant Universe,* chap. 8, on "More Dimensions Than Meet the Eye."

6. Arthur Clarke, *3001: The Final Odyssey* (New York: Ballantine Books, 1997), p. 68.

7. Clarke, *3001,* p. 2.

8. David Brin, *Brightness Reef* (New York: Bantam Books, 1995), pp. 153, 221, 230. Brin posits a sort of species immortality: "[The old ones] vanish from our midst. . . . Some call it transcendence, others call it death" (p. 290).

9. Oscar Cullman, *Immortality of the Soul or Resurrection of the Body?* (London: Epworth Press, 1958), p. 37.

10. Arthur Peacocke, in *Evidence of Purpose,* pp. 102–103. Peacocke summarizes his view of God and time thus: *"God is not 'timeless'; God is temporal in the sense that the Divine life is successive in its relation to us—God is temporarily related to us; God creates and is present to each instant of the (physical and, derivatively, psychological) time of the created world; God transcends past and present time: God is eternal"* (p. x, italics his).

11. Moltmann, *The Coming of God,* pp. 338–339.

CONCLUSION

1. St. Bonaventure, *The Tree of Life,* in *CWS* (New York: Paulist Press, 1978), p. 173.
2. Teilhard de Chardin, *The Divine Milieu* (New York: Harper & Row, 1960), p. 153.
3. John 10:28.
4. Carol Zaleski, *The Life of the World to Come* (New York: Oxford Univ. Press, 1996), p. 67.